Utilization Studies and Residual Measurements

Interagency Technical Reference

Cooperative Extension Service

U.S. Department of Agriculture
—Forest Service—

Natural Resource Conservation Service,
Grazing Land Technology Institute

U.S. Department of the Interior
—Bureau of Land Management—

1996
Revised in 1997, 1999

Supersedes BLM Technical Reference 4400-3, *Utilization Studies*, dated September 1984

Edited, designed, and produced by the Bureau of Land Management's
National Applied Resource Sciences Center

BLM/RS/ST-96/004+1730

UTILIZATION STUDIES AND RESIDUAL MEASUREMENTS

Interagency Technical Reference

By (In alphabetical order)

Bill Coulloudon
Rangeland Management Spec.
Bureau of Land Management
Phoenix, Arizona

Kris Eshelman (deceased)
Rangeland Management Spec.
Bureau of Land Management
Reno, Nevada

James Gianola
Wildhorse and Burro Spec.
Bureau of Land Management
Carson City, Nevada

Ned Habich
Rangeland Management Spec.
Bureau of Land Management
Denver Colorado

Lee Hughes
Ecologist
Bureau of Land Management
St. George, Utah

Curt Johnson
Rangeland Management Spec.
Forest Service Region 4
Ogden Utah

Mike Pellant
Rangeland Ecologist
Bureau of Land Management
Boise, Idaho

Paul Podborny
Wildlife Biologist
Bureau of Land Management
Ely, Nevada

Allen Rasmussen
Rangeland Management Spec.
Cooperative Extension Service
Utah State University
Logan, UT

Ben Robles
Wildlife Biologist
Bureau of Land Management
Safford, Arizona

Pat Shaver
Natural Resource Conservation Service
Rangeland Management Spec.
Corvallis, Oregon

John Spehar
Rangeland Management Spec.
Bureau of Land Management
Rawlins, Wyoming

John Willoughby
State Biologist
Bureau of Land Management
Sacramento, California

Technical Reference 1734-3
copies available from
Bureau of Land Management
National Business Center
BC-650B
P.O. Box 25047
Denver, Colorado 80225-0047

TABLE OF CONTENTS

TABLE OF CONTENTS (continued)

Illustration Number	Title	Page

DEDICATION

This publication is dedicated to the memory of Kristen R. Eshelman, who contributed tremendously to its development and preparation. Throughout his career, Kris was instrumental in producing numerous technical references outlining procedures for rangeland inventory, monitoring, and the evaluation of rangeland data. Through his efforts, resource specialists were provided with the tools to improve the public rangelands for the benefit of rangeland users and the American public.

I. PREFACE

The intent of this interagency monitoring guide is to provide the basis for consistent, uniform, and standard utilization studies and residual measurements that are economical, repeatable, statistically reliable, and technically adequate. While this guide is not all inclusive, it does include the primary study methods used across the West. An omission of a particular sampling method does not mean that the method is not valid in specific locations; it simply means that it is not widely used or recognized throughout the western states. (see Section V.E, Other Methods.)

Proper use and management of our rangeland resources has created a demand for uniformity and consistency in rangeland health measurement methods. As a result of this interest, the USDI Bureau of Land Management (BLM) and USDA Forest Service met in late 1992 and agreed to establish an interagency technical team to jointly oversee the development and publishing of vegetation sampling field guides.

The 13-member team currently includes representatives from the Forest Service, BLM, the Grazing Land Technology Institute of the Natural Resource Conservation Service (NRCS), and the Cooperative Extension Service.

The interagency technical team first met in January 1994 to evaluate the existing rangeland monitoring techniques described in BLM's *Utilization Studies, Technical Reference TR 4400-3.* The team spent 2 years reviewing, modifying, adding to, and eliminating techniques for this interagency Utilization Studies and Residue Measurements technical reference. Feedback from numerous reviewers, including field personnel, resulted in further refinements.

II. INTRODUCTION

Utilization data and residual measurements are important in evaluating the effects of grazing and browsing on rangeland. Utilization measures the percentage of annual herbage production that has been removed. It is generally the percentage of available forage (weight or numbers of plants, twigs, etc.) that has been consumed or destroyed. Utilization is expressed in terms of the current year's production removed. Residual measurement is the determination of herbage material or stubble height left. Residual measurements and utilization data can be used: (1) to identify use patterns, (2) to help establish cause-and-effect interpretations of range trend data, and (3) to aid in adjusting stocking rates when combined with other monitoring data.

Permittees, lessees, other rangeland users, and interested publics should be consulted and encouraged to participate in collecting and analyzing utilization and residual data. Those individual or groups interested in helping to collect data should be trained in the technique used in that specific management unit.

This document deals with the collection of utilization data and residual measurements. The interpretation of this data will be addressed in other documents.

Utilization data and residual measurements should not be used alone to determine stocking rates. Adjustment in stocking rates should also include trend data, climatic information, actual use data, and other information.

A. Terms and Concepts

1. Objectives

a Short-term Use of Utilization Data In the short term, utilization data are considered with actual use and climate data to determine resource use levels and to identify needed adjustments in management actions. These same data can be used in the short term as the basis for adjusting grazing use by agreement or grazing decision.

b Long-term Use of Utilization Data In addition to the above short-term objectives, utilization data are considered along with other monitoring data to determine if management actions or practices are achieving management objectives identified in the land-use, coordinated resource management, and activity plans.

2. Utilization
Utilization is the proportion or degree of current year's forage production that is consumed or destroyed by animals (including insects). Utilization may refer either to a single plant species, a group of species, or the vegetation as a whole. Utilization is synonymous with use. This process requires a comparison of the amount of herbage left compared with the amount of herbage produced during the year.

3. Seasonal Utilization
Seasonal utilization is the amount of utilization that has occurred before the end of the growing season.

4. *Residual Measurements* Residual measurement is the determination of herbage material or stubble height left after a grazing or use period. It is independent of the amount of annual production. Management actions based on stubble height have an impact on plant health and soil and watershed protection because a specified amount of foliage will be left regardless of the amount of annual production. The important management consideration is to determine the species to evaluate and the proper use levels that will leave the appropriate residual stubble height.

5. *Removal Versus Residual* There are two problems with determining utilization or the amount of annual herbage removed: measuring the amount of total production for the year and determining the amount of herbage that has been removed. Measuring the residual plant biomass or stubble height rather than utilization may be preferable because it is the plant biomass remaining that will have an important impact on plant health, potential regrowth, and soil and watershed protection.

B. Guidelines

The techniques described here are guidelines for establishing and conducting utilization and residue studies. They are not standards. Utilization and residue sampling techniques and standards need to be based on management objectives. Techniques can be modified or adjusted to fit a particular resource situation or management objectives as long as the principles of the technique are maintained. Before a modified technique is used, it should be reviewed by agency monitoring coordinators, cooperators, and other qualified individuals. A modified technique should be clearly identified and labeled as "**MODIFIED.**" All modifications to transect layout, etc., should be clearly documented each time the method is used.

If at all possible, utilization and residue studies should be established not only to determine the amount of use occurring, but also to determine the agent (livestock, wildlife, insects, recreation, etc.) causing the use.

C. Location of Sample Sites

Utilization and residue studies can be completed anywhere, depending on the objectives. For use pattern mapping, utilization and residue studies should be collected on enough sites to provide a clear picture of the use that has occurred.

The site selection process used should be documented. Documentation should include the management objectives, the criteria used for selecting the sites, and the kinds of comparisons or interpretations expected to be made from them.

Common locations for studies include critical areas and key areas. Some of the site characteristics and other information that may be considered in the selecting study sites are:

- Soil
- Vegetation (kinds and distribution of plants)
- Ecological sites
- Seral stage
- Topography
- Location of water, fences, and natural barriers
- Size of pasture

- Kind and/or class of forage animals - livestock, wildlife, wild horses, and wild burros
- Habits of the animals, including foraging
- Areas of animal concentration
- Location and extent of critical areas
- Erosion conditions
- Threatened, endangered, and sensitive species - both plant and animal
- Periods of animal use
- Grazing history
- Location of salt, mineral, and protein supplements
- Location of livestock, wildlife, wild horse, and/or wild burro trails

1. *Critical Areas* Critical areas are areas that should be evaluated separately from the remainder of a management unit because they contain special or unique values. Critical areas could include fragile watersheds, sage grouse nesting grounds, riparian areas, areas of critical environmental concern, etc.

2. *Key Areas* Key areas are indicator areas that are able to reflect what is happening on a larger area as a result of on-the-ground management actions. A key area should be a representative sample of a large stratum, such as a pasture, grazing allotment, wildlife habitat area, herd management area, watershed area, etc., depending on the management objectives being addressed by the study. Key areas represent the "pulse" of the rangeland. Proper selection of key areas requires appropriate stratification. Statistical inference can only be applied to the stratification unit.

   a **Selecting Key Areas** The most important factors to consider when selecting key areas are the management objectives found in land use plans, coordinated resource management plans, and/or activity plans. An interdisciplinary team should be used to select these areas. In addition, permittees, lessees, and other interested publics should be invited to participate, as appropriate, in selecting key areas. Poor information resulting from improper selection of key areas leads to misguided decisions and improper management.

   b **Criteria for Selecting Key Areas** The following are some criteria that should be considered in selecting key areas. A key area:

   - Should be representative of the stratum in which it is located.

   - Should be located within a single ecological site and plant community.

   - Should contain the key species where the key species concept is used.

   - Should be capable of, and likely to show, a response to management actions. This response should be indicative of the response that is occurring on the stratum.

   c **Number of Key Areas** The number of key areas selected to represent a stratum ideally depends on the size of the stratum and on data needs. However, the number of areas may ultimately be limited by funding and personnel constraints.

d Objectives Objectives should be developed so that they are specific to the key area. Monitoring studies can then be designed to determine if these objectives are being met.

e Mapping Key Areas Key areas should be accurately delineated on aerial photos and/or maps. Mapping of key areas will provide a permanent record of their location.

D. Key Species
Key species are generally an important component of a plant community. Key species serve as indicators of change and may or may not be forage species. More than one key species may be selected for a stratum, depending on management objectives and data needs. In some cases, problem plants (poisonous, exotics, etc.) may be selected as key species. Key species may change from season to season and year to year.

1. *Selecting Key Species* Selection of key species should be tied directly to management objectives in land use, coordinated resource management, and activity plans. The species selected will depend upon the plant species in the present plant community, the present ecological status, and the potential natural communities for the specific sites. An interdisciplinary team should be used in selecting key species to ensure that data needs of the various resources are met. In addition, interested publics should be invited to participate, as appropriate, in selecting these species.

2. *Considerations in Selecting Key Species* The following points should be considered in selecting key species:

   a The forage value of key species may be of secondary or no importance. For example, watershed protection may require selection of plants as key species that protect the watershed but are not the best forage species. In some cases, threatened, endangered, or sensitive species that have no particular forage value may be selected as key species.

   b Any foraging use of the key species on key areas is assumed to reflect foraging use on the entire stratum. Utilization percentages in this situation are an index of the use on key species.

   c Depending on the selected management strategy and/or periods of use, key species may be foraged during the growing period, after maturity, or both.

   d In areas of yearlong grazing use and in areas where there is more than one use period, several key species may be selected. For example, on an area with both spring and summer grazing use, a cool season plant may be the key species during the spring, while a warm season plant may be the key species during the summer.

   e Selection of several key species may be desirable when adjustments in livestock grazing use are anticipated. This is especially true if more than one plant species contributes a major portion of the forage base of the animals using the area (Smith 1965).

3. *Key Species on Depleted Rangelands* The key species selected should be present on each study site on which utilization and residue studies are conducted; however, on depleted rangelands these species may be sparse. In this situation it may be necessary to conduct monitoring studies on other species. Data gathered on non-key species must be interpreted on the basis of effects on the establishment and subsequent response of the key species. It should also be verified that the site is ecologically capable of producing the key species.

E. Coordination

Utilization and residue studies should be planned and implemented on an interdisciplinary basis. Coordination with livestock operators, other appropriate state and federal agencies, and interested publics is also a crucial factor to success.

F. Electronic Data Recorders

Electronic data recorders are handheld "computers" that are constructed to withstand the harsh environmental conditions found in the field. They are used to record monitoring data in a digital format that can be transferred directly to a personal computer for storage and retrieval. They require minimal maintenance, are generally programmable, and allow easy data entry using a wand and bar codes.

Recording field data using an electronic data recorder takes approximately the same amount of time as using printed forms. The advantage with electronic data recorders is that they improve efficiency by reducing errors associated with entering data into a computer for analysis. They can also reduce the time needed for data compilation and summarization.

The cost of electronic data recorders and computer software programs is considerable and should be evaluated prior to purchase. It is also important to have good computer support assistance available to help users in operating, downloading, and troubleshooting electronic data recorders, especially during the initial use period.

III. STUDY DESIGN AND ANALYSIS

The rangeland monitoring methods described in Section V have a number of common elements. Those that relate to permanently marking and documenting the study location are described in detail below.

Also discussed in this section are statistical considerations (target populations, random sampling, systematic sampling, confidence intervals, etc.) and other important factors (properly identifying plant species and training people so they follow the correct procedures).

It is important to read this chapter before referring to the specific methods described in Section V, since the material covered here will not be repeated for each of them.

- *Permanently Marking the Study Location* Permanently mark the location of each study by means of a reference post (steel post) placed about 100 feet from the actual study location. Record the bearing and distance from the post to the study location. An alternative is to select a reference point, such as a prominent natural or manmade feature, and record the bearing and distance from that point to the study location. If a post is used, it should be tagged to indicate that it marks the location of a monitoring study and should not be disturbed.

  Permanently mark the study location itself by driving angle iron stakes into the ground at randomly selected starting points. The baseline technique requires that both ends of the baseline be permanently staked. If the linear technique is used, only the beginning point of the study needs to be permanently staked. Establish the study according to the directions found in Section III.A.2 beginning on the next page.

  Paint the study location stake with brightly colored permanent spray paint (yellow or orange) to aid in relocation. Repaint this stake when subsequent readings are made.

- *Study Documentation* Document the study and transect locations, number of transects, starting points, bearings, length, distance between transects, number of observation points, sampling interval, and other pertinent information concerning a study on the Study Location and Documentation Data form (see Appendix A). Plot the precise location of the studies on detailed maps and/or aerial photos.

  For transects that use a baseline technique, record the location of each transect or quadrat along the baseline and the direction (left or right). Be sure to document the exact location of the study and the directions for relocating. For example: *1.2 miles from the allotment boundary fence on the Old County Line Road. The reference post is on the south side of the road, 50 feet from the road.*

A. **Planning the Study** Proper planning is by far the most important part of a utilization or residue study. Much wasted time and effort can be avoided by proper planning. A few important considerations are discussed below. The reader should refer to the Technical Reference, *Measuring & Monitoring Plant Populations,* for a more complete discussion of these important steps.

   1. *Identify Objectives* Based on land use and activity plans, identify management objectives appropriate for the area to be monitored. The intent is to evaluate the

effects of management actions on achieving management objectives by collecting utilization or residual data.

2. *Design the Study* The number of points, quadrats, or transects (sample size) needed depends on the monitoring objectives and the efficiency of the sampling design. It should be known *before* beginning the study how the data will be analyzed. The frequency of data collection (e.g., every year, every other year, etc.) and data sheet design should be determined before studies are implemented. The sample data sheets included with each method (following the narrative) are only examples of data forms. Field offices have the option to modify these forms or develop their own.

All methods described in this document can be established using either the linear or baseline design.

a **Linear** This study design samples a management units or study site in a straight line (Figure 1). Randomly select the beginning point of the transect within the management units or study site. The transect site can be permanently marked with a transect location stake, if needed. Randomly determine the transect bearing and select a prominent distant landmark such as a peak, rocky point, etc., that can be used as the transect bearing point. Utilization and residue readings are taken at a specified interval (paced or measured) along the transect bearing. If the examiner is unable to collect an adequate sample with this transect before leaving the study site, additional transects can be run from the transect location stake at different bearings.

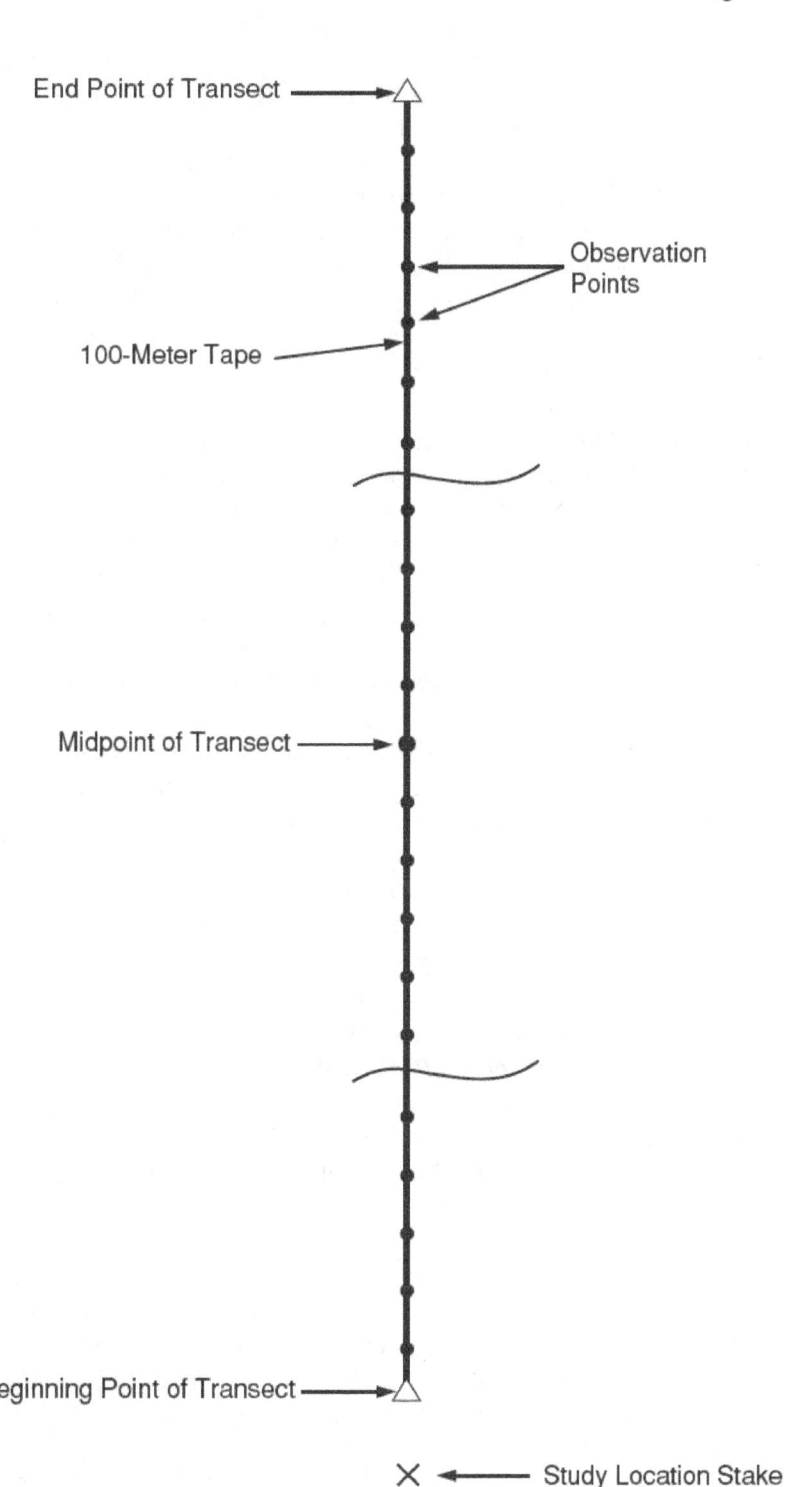

Figure 1. Study layout for the linear technique.

b Baseline A baseline is established by stretching a tape measure of any desired length between two stakes (Figure 2). For an extremely long baseline, intermediate stakes can be used to ensure proper alignment. It is recommended that metric measurement be used. Individual transects are then run perpendicular to the baseline at random locations along the tape. Transects can all be run in the same direction, in which case the baseline forms one of the outer boundaries of the sampled area, or in two directions, in which case the baseline runs through the center of the sampled area. If transects are run in two directions, the direction for each individual transect should be determined randomly. (Directions on the use of random number tables and random number generators are given in Appendix F.) Observation points are spaced at specified distances along the transect. This study design is intended to randomly sample a specified area. The area to be sampled can be expanded as necessary by lengthening the baseline and/or increasing the length between sampling points.

B. Statistical Considerations

1. *Target Population* Sample sites are selected (subjectively) that hopefully reflect what is happening on a larger area. These may be study sites that are considered to be representative of a larger area (such as a pasture) or may be critical areas such as sites where endangered species occur (see Section II.C). Utilization and residue studies are then located on these sites. Since study sites are subjectively selected, no valid statistical projections to an entire management area are possible. Therefore, careful consideration and good professional judgement must be used in selecting study sites to ensure the validity of any conclusions reached.

   a Although it would be convenient to make inferences regarding larger areas from sampling study sites, there is no way this can be done in the statistical sense because these study sites have been chosen subjectively.

   b For this reason it is important to develop objectives that are specific to study sites. It is equally important to make it clear what actions will be taken based on what happens on the study sites.

   c It is also important to base objectives and management actions on each study site separately. *Values from study sites from different strata should never be averaged.*

   d From a sampling perspective, it is the study sites that constitutes the *target population*. The collection of all possible sampling units that could be placed in the study sites is the target population.

2. *Random Sampling* Critical to valid monitoring study design is that the sample be drawn randomly from the population of interest. There are several methods of random sampling, several of which are discussed briefly below, but the important point is that all of the statistical analysis techniques available are based on knowing the probability of selecting a particular sampling unit. If some type of random selection of sampling units is not incorporated into the study design, the probability of selection cannot be determined and no statistical inferences can be made about the population. (Directions on the use of random number tables and random number generators are given in Appendix F.)

Study Layout

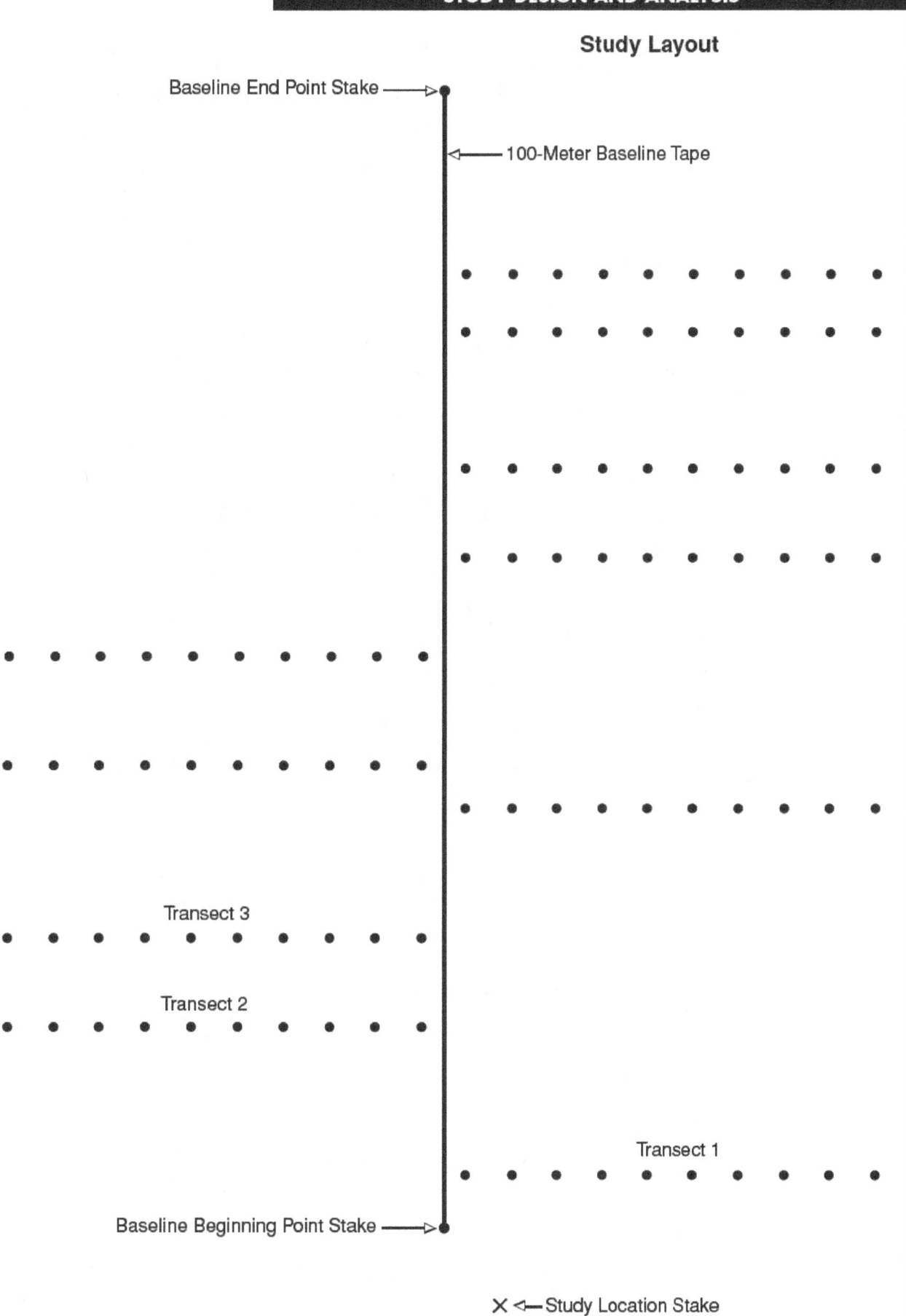

Figure 2. Study layout for the baseline technique.

3. *Systematic Sampling* Systematic sampling is very common in utilization and residue studies. The collection of utilization or residual data along a transect at specified intervals is an example of systematic sampling. The starting point of a transect must be randomly selected. If the interval between observations is 5 paces (meters or feet can be used), a number between 0 and 4 is randomly selected to represent the distance from the reference point or baseline to start making observations. Additional observations are made at 5-pace intervals from this starting point. Thus, if 10 observations are to be made at 5-pace intervals and the randomly selected number between 0 and 4 is 2, then the first observation is made at 2 paces and the remaining observations occur at 7, 12, 17, 22, 27, 32, 37, 42, and 47 paces along the transect.

Strictly speaking, systematic sampling is analogous to simple random sampling only when the population being sampled is in random order (see, for example, Williams 1978). Many natural populations of both plants and animals exhibit an aggregated (also called clumped) spatial distribution pattern. This means that nearby units tend to be similar to (correlated with) each other. If, in a systematic sample, the sampling units are spaced far enough apart to reduce this correlation, the systematic sample will tend to furnish a better average and smaller standard error than is the case with a random sample, because with a completely random sample one is more likely to end up with at least some sampling units close together (see Milne 1959 and the discussion of sampling an ordered population in Scheaffer et al. 1979).

4. *Sampling Versus Nonsampling Errors* In any monitoring study, it pays to keep the error rate as low as possible. Errors can be separated into sampling errors and nonsampling errors.

   a **Sampling Errors** Sampling errors arise from chance variation; they do not result from "mistakes" such as misidentifying a species. They occur when the sample does not reflect the true population. The magnitude of sampling errors *can* be measured.

   b **Nonsampling Errors** Nonsampling errors are "mistakes" that cannot be measured.

   Examples of nonsampling errors:

   - Using biased selection rules, such as selecting "representative samples" by subjectively locating sampling units or substituting sampling units that are "easier" to measure.

   - Sloppy field work.

   - Transcription and recording errors.

   - Incorrect or inconsistent species identification.

   To minimizing nonsampling errors:

   - When different personnel are used, conduct rigorous training and testing to ensure consistency in measurement and estimation.

- Design field forms that are easy to use and not confusing to data transcribers. Double- or triple-check all data entered into computer programs to ensure the numbers are correct.

5. *Confidence Interval* In rangeland monitoring, the true population total (or any other true population parameter) can never be determined. The best way to judge how well a sample estimates the true population total is by calculating a *confidence interval*. The confidence interval is a range of values that is expected to include the true population size (or any other parameter of interest, often an average) a given percentage of the time (Krebs 1989). Confidence intervals are the principal means of analyzing utilization data. For instructions in calculating confidence intervals, see the Technical Reference, *Measuring & Monitoring Plant Populations*.

6. *Interspersion* One of the most important considerations of sampling is good interspersion of sampling units throughout the area to be sampled (the target population). The basic goal should be to have sampling units as well interspersed throughout the area of the target population as possible. The practice of placing all of the sampling units, whether they be quadrats or points, along a single transect or even a few transects should be avoided. Arranging sampling units in this manner results in poor interspersion of sampling units and makes it unlikely that the sample will provide a representative sample of the target population. This is true even if the single transect or few transects are randomly located.

7. *Pilot Studies* In several places in this chapter, the need to conduct pilot studies has been stressed. The principal purpose of pilot studies is to determine the sample size necessary to estimate vegetation characteristics of interest (e.g., utilization level, stubble height, biomass) with a given level of precision. Pilot sampling allows the examiner to obtain stable estimates of the population average and the population standard deviation. This is accomplished by using standard deviation calculations and sequential sampling as described below.

   a **Standard Deviation Calculations** The following shows how to calculate the standard deviation for utilization on sideoats grama. The standard deviation is calculated as follows:

$$S = \sqrt{\frac{(X_1 - \overline{X})^2 + (X_2 - \overline{X})^2 + \ldots + (X_n - \overline{X})^2}{n-1}} \quad or \quad S = \sqrt{\frac{\sum (X - \overline{X})^2}{n-1}}$$

where:

S = standard deviation
X = number of plants
$\overline{X}$ = the mean or average % utilization or residual measurement
n = the number of samples (observation points in this example)

Utilization estimates	Deviation $(X - \overline{X})$	Squared Deviation $(X - \overline{X})^2$
49	49-39 = 10	100
37	37-39 = -2	4
39	39-39 = 0	0
49	49-39 = 10	100
22	22-39 = -17	289
$\overline{X}$= 196/5 = 39		493

$$S = \sqrt{\frac{\Sigma (X - \overline{X})^2}{n-1}} = \sqrt{\frac{493}{5-1}} = \sqrt{\frac{493}{4}} = \sqrt{123} = 11.10$$

b **Sequential Sampling** The estimate of the standard deviation derived through pilot sampling is one of the values used to calculate sample size, whether one uses the formulas given in the Technical Reference, *Measuring & Monitoring Plant Populations*, or a computer program. Sequential sampling helps determine whether the examiner has taken a large enough pilot sample to use the standard deviation from the pilot sample to calculate sample size. The process is accomplished as follows.

Gather pilot sampling data using some arbitrarily selected sample size. Calculate the average and standard deviation for the first two sampling units (for the methods described in this Technical Reference these are either individual plants, quadrats, or observation points), calculate it again after putting in the next sampling unit value, and continue these iterative calculations after the addition of each sampling unit value to the sample. This will generate a running average and standard deviation. Look at the four columns of numbers on the left of Figure 3.

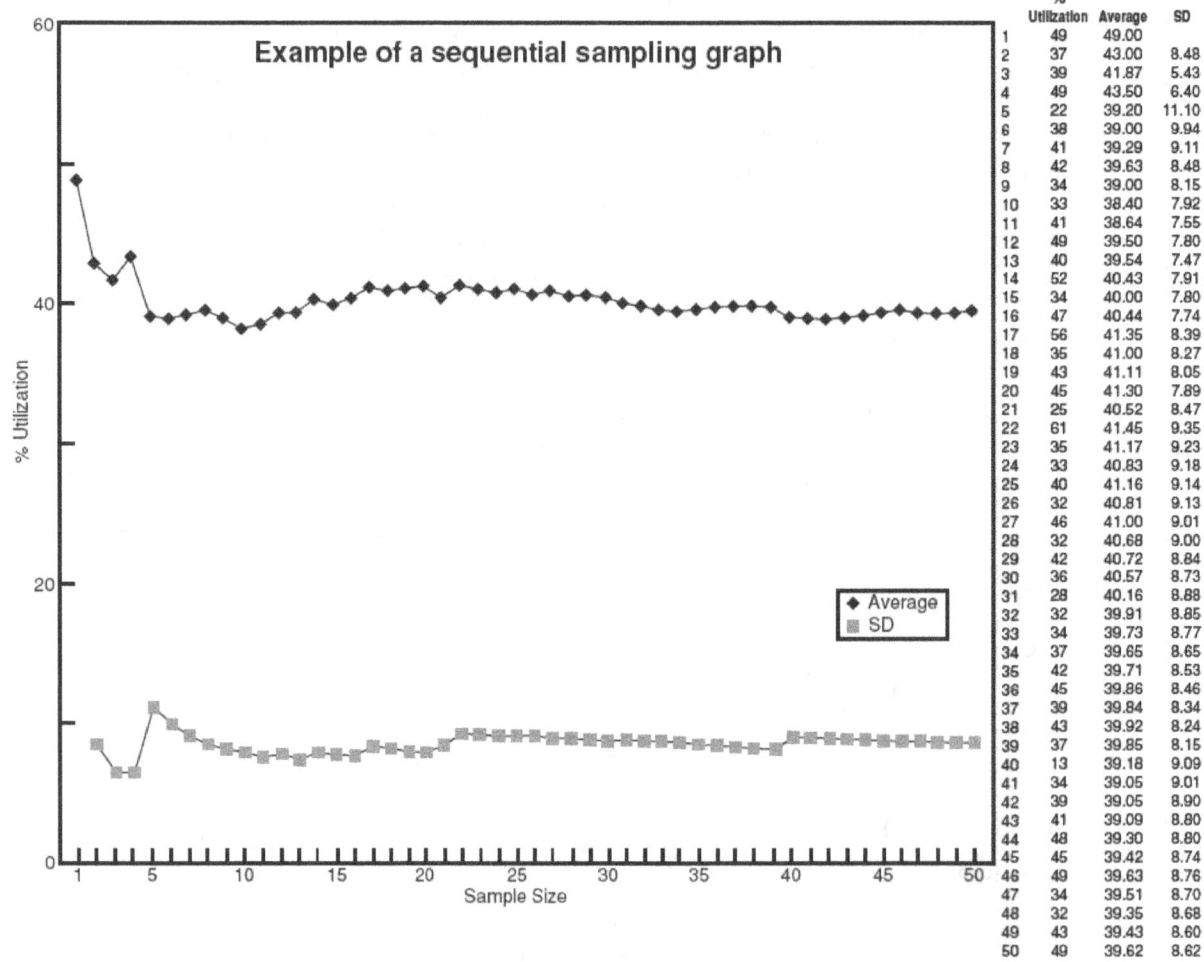

	% Utilization	Average	SD
1	49	49.00	
2	37	43.00	8.48
3	39	41.87	5.43
4	49	43.50	6.40
5	22	39.20	11.10
6	38	39.00	9.94
7	41	39.29	9.11
8	42	39.63	8.48
9	34	39.00	8.15
10	33	38.40	7.92
11	41	38.64	7.55
12	49	39.50	7.80
13	40	39.54	7.47
14	52	40.43	7.91
15	34	40.00	7.80
16	47	40.44	7.74
17	56	41.35	8.39
18	35	41.00	8.27
19	43	41.11	8.05
20	45	41.30	7.89
21	25	40.52	8.47
22	61	41.45	9.35
23	35	41.17	9.23
24	33	40.83	9.18
25	40	41.16	9.14
26	32	40.81	9.13
27	46	41.00	9.01
28	32	40.68	9.00
29	42	40.72	8.84
30	36	40.57	8.73
31	28	40.16	8.88
32	32	39.91	8.85
33	34	39.73	8.77
34	37	39.65	8.65
35	42	39.71	8.53
36	45	39.86	8.46
37	39	39.84	8.34
38	43	39.92	8.24
39	37	39.85	8.15
40	13	39.18	9.09
41	34	39.05	9.01
42	39	39.05	8.90
43	41	39.09	8.80
44	48	39.30	8.80
45	45	39.42	8.74
46	49	39.63	8.76
47	34	39.51	8.70
48	32	39.35	8.68
49	43	39.43	8.60
50	49	39.62	8.62

Figure 3. Example of a sequential sampling graph. The running average and standard deviation are plotted for sample sizes up to n=50. Data are utilization percentages calculated using the paired plot method. Actual values are shown on the left. As this graph shows, both the average and the standard deviation have stabilized by about n=23. The standard deviation at n=23 (9.23) can be plugged into a sample-size formula to determine the sample size needed for estimating the utilization with the precision specified.

Plot on graph paper (or use a computer program to plot) the sample size versus the average and standard deviation. Look for curves smoothing out. In the example shown in Figure 3, the curves smooth out after n = 21-25. The decision to stop sampling is a subjective one. There are no hard-and-fast rules.

A computer is valuable for creating sequential sampling graphs. Spreadsheet programs such as Lotus 1-2-3 allow for both entering the data in a form that can be analyzed later and simultaneously creating a sequential sampling graph of the running average and standard deviation. This also allows one to look at several random sequences of the data before deciding on the number of sampling units to measure.

Use the sequential sampling method to determine what sample size *not* to use (don't use the sample size below the point where the running average and standard deviation have not stabilized). Plug the final average and standard deviation information into the appropriate sample size equation to determine the optimum sample size.

c **Sample Size Determination** An adequate sample is vital to the success of any successful monitoring effort. Adequacy relates to the ability of the observer to evaluate whether the management objective has been achieved. Management objectives related to utilization, for example, will state maximum allowable levels of utilization on key species. Thus, the management objective might be to allow utilization of no more than 30 percent on key species X. Because the utilization of all plants of key species X cannot be measured, a sample must be taken. Depending upon how large a sample is taken and how variable the utilization is in the area sampled, the estimate from the sample may be very close to the true value or very far from it. The confidence interval in the former case will be narrow; in the latter case it will be wide.

The first step in determining sample size is to take the management objective and frame a corresponding monitoring objective. This monitoring objective specifies how precise an estimate is needed to assess whether the management objective has been met. In the example introduced above, our management objective is as follows:

Allow no more than 30 percent utilization of Key Species X in study site Y in any year.

The corresponding monitoring objective might be:

Estimate the utilization on Key Species X in study site Y every year. Ensure, with 95 percent confidence, that the estimate is within 5 percent (absolute) of the true utilization value.

Note that this monitoring objective has specified a 95 percent confidence interval size of ±5 percent for the estimate. This means that if the average from the sample is 25 percent utilization on the key species, the examiner can be 95 percent confident that the true amount of utilization on the key species throughout the area sampled is somewhere between 20 percent and 30 percent.

Once the monitoring objective has been developed and there is a good estimate of the standard deviation derived from sequential sampling, the sample size needed to meet this monitoring objective can be calculated. Formulas for calculating sample sizes are given in the Technical Reference, *Measuring & Monitoring Plant Populations*. Because these formulas are rather unwieldy, you may choose to use a computer program. There are at least two computer programs that will calculate the sample size necessary to estimate a single population average with a given level of precision. These are the program DESIGN (by SYSTAT) and PC-SIZE: CONSULTANT. Both of these were developed by Gerard E. Dallal, but the latter is a much better value, since it is shareware (the author asks for a fee of $15.00 if the user finds the program to be useful). The program is available via the World Wide Web at the following address:

http://www.coast.net/SimTel/SimTel/

Once at the homepage, change to the directory msdos/statstic/ and download the file st-size.zip. Unzip the file using the shareware program PKUNZIP. Executable files and documentation are included.

Consult the Technical Reference, *Measuring & Monitoring Plant Populations*, for more information on calculating sample size.

8. *Graphical Display of Data* The use of graphs, both to initially explore the quality of the monitoring data collected and to display the results of the data analysis, is important to designing and implementing monitoring studies. See the Technical Reference, *Measuring & Monitoring Plant Populations*, for descriptions of these graphs, along with examples.

a **Graphs to Examine Study Data Prior to Analysis** The best of these graphs plot each data point. These graphs can help determine whether the data meet the assumptions of parametric statistics, or whether the data set contains outliers (data with values much lower or much higher than most of the rest of the data — as might occur if one made a mistake in measuring or recording). Normal probability plots and box plots are two of the most useful types for this purpose. For more information, see the Technical Reference, *Measuring & Monitoring Plant Populations*.

b **Graphs to Display the Results of Data Analysis** Rather than displaying each data point, these graphs display summary statistics (e.g., averages, totals, or proportions). When these summary statistics are graphed, error bars must be used to display the precision of estimates. Because it is the true parameter (average or median) that is of interest, confidence intervals should be used as error bars. Types of graphs include:

(1) Bar charts of averages or medians with confidence intervals.

(2) Graphs of summary statistics plotted as points, with error bars.

(3) Box plots with "notches" for error bars.

9. *Data Analysis and Interpretation* Utilization and residue studies do not compare data differences between years, so significance tests are not ordinarily employed. The appropriate analysis of utilization data depends upon whether management objectives are written based on the average, median, or other

percentile utilization. Confidence intervals (for a selected level of confidence) are then calculated around this average, median, or other percentile.

Confidence intervals are set around an estimated average value to indicate that the true average of the population will occur within those limits a specified percentage of the time. The sample average is the best estimate of the population average available if it has been measured in an unbiased way. (The confidence interval does not account for bias, which arises from error or incompetence.) The width of the confidence interval is determined by the variability of the measurements.

For many utilization objectives, the median is a better measure of central tendency than the average. This is particularly true for stubble height data, where the average should never be used as the measure of central tendency. Using the median ensures that at least half of the plants measured meet or exceed whatever objective has been set. Because utilization data are often not normally distributed, using the average will not guarantee this. Just as with the average, confidence intervals for the median must be calculated.

Another alternative is to base the management objective on a percentile other than the median (the median is the 50th percentile). For example, with stubble height data the objective could be that at least 60 percent of the plants be taller than a selected threshold, say 4 inches. A confidence interval would then be constructed around the 60th percentile of the sample data and the lower bound of the interval used as the conservative estimate of the true 60th percentile. For example, the sample 60th percentile may be 4.5 inches and the 95 percent confidence interval for the 60th percentile may be 3.75 inches to 5.25 inches. The 3.75-inch figure would be used as the conservative estimate of the 60th percentile.

C. Collecting Utilization Data and Residue Measurements

1. *Transects* Utilization and residue studies should be located within representative portions of the management unit (see Section II.C).

   a **Starting Point** The starting point of a transect should be randomly located.

   b **Bearing or Direction** The bearing or direction of the transect from the starting point should either be set by compass or directed toward a permanent, clearly defined, highly visible natural feature. Straight-line transects should cross drainages, if possible, in order to obtain a representative sample. Where uplands and riparian areas have significantly different levels of utilization, they should not be included within the same study site since extremes in percent utilization on one portion of the site may mask extremes on other portions of the site. See Section III.A.2 for a discussion on establishing a baseline technique for collecting utilization data.

2. *Observations and Quadrats*

   a **Sampling Interval** Observations or quadrats are located at constant intervals along transects. If the key species or other selected species is not present at the selected interval, relocate the observation point or quadrat to the nearest individual of that species along each transect line. The next interval along each transect is measured from this relocated point.

b **Observation Sites** Exercise care to ensure that observation sites do not overlap.

c **Quadrat Size** If quadrats are used, ensure that all quadrats on a transect are of the same size so that the individual quadrat percentages can be added together and averaged.

d **Number of Observations or Quadrats** Use pilot transects to determine the number of observation points or quadrats. Inaccuracies produced by estimating utilization tend to be reduced by using a larger number of observations or quadrats.

e **Statistical Analysis** Run statistical analysis on pilot (sample) transects to assure adequate sample size and required precision (see Section III.B.7).

f **Marking Locations** Record the location of each transect on a map or aerial photo.

3. *Frequency of Studies* Utilization and residue studies may be conducted every year or as often as needed after the growing season to satisfy data requirements for grazing allotment, wildlife habitat area, herd management area, watershed area, or other designated management area evaluations. In some cases, utilization and residue studies are started upon initiation of intensive management and continued annually through one complete cycle of a grazing system, or for as long as necessary. It may be necessary to conduct utilization and residue studies annually until management objectives are achieved and maintained. Utilization and residue studies may also be conducted at periodic intervals in sequence with grazing treatments. For example, utilization and residue studies on individual pastures could be conducted once every three years on a three pasture grazing system and once every five years on a five-pasture grazing system. Where studies are conducted only once during each grazing cycle, they should be conducted at the same point in each cycle so that the data will be comparable.

4. *Timing of Studies* Utilization studies are conducted at the end of the growing period within pastures or management units. Seasonal utilization studies are generally conducted at the end of each period of use within pastures or management units. They may also be conducted at any time during the period of use. Where livestock, wildlife, wild horses, and/or wild burros are present, it may be necessary to conduct seasonal utilization studies both before and after discrete periods of use by these animals to estimate the percent utilization by kind of animal. Where regrowth may occur, seasonal utilization studies should be conducted as soon as possible following the end of the period of use. Utilization studies on browse species must be conducted before new twig growth occurs to obtain accurate measurements or observations of past use.

5. *Documentation* Utilization data are recorded on appropriate forms. Forms for the methods described in this Technical Reference are included in the section describing the method. Close-up and/or general view photographs may be used with any of the methods (see Section V.A in the Interagency Technical Reference,

Sampling Vegetation Attributes). File the forms, photographs, and any other pertinent information in the monitoring file or as otherwise prescribed.

6. *Interpreting Utilization and Residue Data*

a Utilization is an important factor that can bring about changes in soil, water, animal, and vegetation resources. The impact that a specific intensity of use has on a plant species is highly variable, depending on past and present use, period of use, duration of use, interspecies competition, weather, availability of soil moisture for regrowth, and how these factors interact. Utilization and residue data can be used alone to determine when livestock should be moved within a grazing allotment and to identify livestock distribution problems. In combination with actual use and climatic data, utilization and residue measurements and utilization pattern mapping are useful for estimating proper stocking levels under current management. Utilization and residue studies are also helpful in identifying key, critical, and problem areas, and in identifying range improvements needed to improve livestock distribution.

b When interpreting utilization and residue data, it is important to consider the climatic conditions that have occurred during the growing season. Light grazing use during a drought year can appear to be the same as heavy use during a normal or above-average precipitation year.

c The reaction that plants have to different levels of utilization can depend on past conditions and use. Plants that have been rested for a short time, even during a drought period, can deal with heavier use better than plants that have been previously stressed by heavy use.

d The relationship between the level of utilization and the overall condition of the plant is not always clear. Climatic conditions, composition of adjacent vegetation, season of use and other variables must be taken into account in interpreting utilization and residual studies (Sharp et al. 1994).

D. Other Important Considerations Consistency is important in measuring or estimating utilization.

1. *Availability* The measurement of forage utilization should be based on the availability of the vegetation. Vegetation that is beyond the reach of grazing animals because of obstructions such as brush or height should not be considered in determining the level of utilization.

2. *Plant Species Identification* It is important that the plant species be properly identified when conducting utilization and residue studies. In some cases, it may be helpful to include pressed plant specimens, photographs, or other aids used for species identification in the study file. If data are collected prior to positive species identification, examiners should collect plant specimens for later verification.

3. *Utilization Levels* "Desired," or "target," utilization levels for specific areas of rangeland are reflected in the management objectives of land-use, coordinated resource management, and activity plans. These levels refer to the desired utilization of key plant species or several plant species within a study site. The desired

percent utilization for a plant species can vary from plant community to plant community. It can also vary depending on period of use, previous intensity of use, and growth conditions or vigor of the plants. Other demands, such as concurrent or seasonal use by more than one animal species, may also be important in selecting the desired utilization level. Percent utilization is expressed in terms of plant species and locality.

4. *Plants Used to Determine Utilization* Generally, only plants of the selected key species are used in utilization and residue studies. This does not preclude sampling plants of other species if these additional data are needed.

5. *Plant Height-Weight Relationship* Weight is not evenly distributed throughout the height or length of plants of any given species. For most rangeland plants, a high percentage of the weight is in the basal portion of the plant or twig where growth is thicker or more dense. A low percentage of plant weight is in the upper portion where growth is tapered or less dense. When estimating percent utilization, adjust for differences in weight by height or length. Weight distribution in relation to height is reasonably constant among individuals of the same plant species.

6. *Utilization Cages* Utilization cages are used to provide a guide to utilization and production. Grasses, forbs, and shrubs can be protected from foraging with these cages. Utilization cages should not appreciably disrupt normal vegetation growth. The cages must be moved each year at the beginning of the foraging period. This will allow for comparison of rangelands inside and outside the protected plots. These cages can be used to show utilization rates to all interested parties. They can also be used to collect information showing forage production fluctuations due to yearly climatic changes (see Section V.C.1 and Appendix E).

7. *Regrowth* Plant regrowth occurs following an interruption in growth by grazing, fire, etc., as well as growth that occurs in response to favorable weather events following the normal growing season. When animals use the same area more than once a year and plant regrowth may occur or has occurred, seasonal utilization is based on the amount of growth available at the time the data are collected. The percent seasonal utilization after each period of use represents only the amount of available growth that has been utilized up to the time the studies are conducted. Seasonal utilization percentages recorded for various periods of use during a year cannot simply be added together to get total utilization for the year. In other words, 30 percent seasonal utilization of 6 inches of plant growth available in the spring, and 30 percent seasonal utilization of 12 inches of plant growth available in the fall, do not add up to 60 percent utilization for the year.

8. *Study Site Assessment* The effectiveness of ecosystem management may require the collection of utilization data on more than the key livestock forage species. Each site selected for completion of utilization and residue studies should be evaluated to determine what plant species are being utilized. It is important to consider use by all animals: livestock, wildlife, and insects. Nonconsumptive uses such as trampling and damage from recreational activities should also be analyzed.

The length of the growing season can affect the species to be evaluated. It is important to determine whether a study site supports both cool and warm season species. It may be necessary to collect utilization data on both cool season and warm season species at different times during the year to get a complete picture of grazing impacts on ecosystem management.

9. *Training* The objective of training is to provide examiners with the skills needed to implement utilization and residue studies and collect reliable, unbiased, and consistent data. Examiners should understand procedures for data collection, data recording, study location documentation, and data analysis, interpretation, and evaluation. Examiners should also be taught the importance of uniformity, accuracy, and reliability in collecting monitoring data. Examiners must be able to accurately identify plant species.

   Training should occur in the field by qualified personnel to ensure that examiners are familiar with the equipment and supplies and that detailed procedural instructions are thoroughly demonstrated and understood.

   As a follow-up to the training, utilization data collected should be examined early in the effort to ensure that the data are properly collected and recorded.

   Periodic review and/or recalibration during the field season may be necessary for maintaining consistency among examiners because of progressive phenological changes. Review and recalibration during each field season are especially important where data collection methods require estimates rather than direct measurements.

IV. UTILIZATION PATTERNS (USE ZONES)

Rangelands include various combinations of range sites and vegetation types on which utilization is seldom uniform. Utilization patterns (use zones) may result from a number of factors that either alone or in combination cause foraging animals to concentrate in specific areas or to spread out over large areas.

For mapping use zones, any number of use classes can be identified based on need. The seven class delineation described in the Keys Species Method (0-5%, 6-20%, 21-40%, 41-60%, 61-80%, 81-94%, 95-100%) as well as a three class delineation (0-40%, 41-60%, 61-100%) are often used.

A. Base Map for Displaying Utilization Patterns
Aerial photographs, ortho-photo quads, or topographic maps should be used for mapping utilization patterns. It is important that the selected base show ecological sites or vegetation types and physical features such as fences, water, and roads. If utilization patterns are mapped on mylar overlayed on a base map, the patterns can easily be compared between years. Geographic information systems can also be used for this purpose.

B. Mapping Utilization Patterns
Utilization patterns may be mapped for wildlife, wild horses, or wild burros, as well as for livestock, following discrete use periods by these animals.

The first step in conducting utilization studies is preparing a map that shows the forage utilization patterns in a pasture or management unit. Mapping utilization patterns involves traversing the management unit or pasture to obtain a general concept of these patterns. Mapping proceeds as the pasture is traversed. When another use zone is observed, the approximate boundary of the zone is recorded on the map. Areas that do not have any of the key species should also be delineated. Information that should be recorded for each traversed use zone include the name(s) of the key or important plant species grazed. Features such as topography, rockiness, size of the area, location of salt, and distance from water all affect foraging habits of different kinds of animals. Recording signs of use by wildlife, wild horses and burros, or livestock in an area can be useful for determining the kinds of large herbivores using an area. Unused areas suitable for grazing and areas of animal concentration should be delineated to help identify range improvements needed to change grazing use distribution. Mapped utilization patterns can be used to stratify a management unit or pasture and to select key areas. Permittees, lessees, other rangeland users, and interested parties should be consulted and encouraged to participate in the mapping of utilization patterns.

Documentation of livestock and wildlife use during a use period is beneficial for observing use patterns as they develop.

The standard time for preparing use mapping and completing utilization measurement should be at the end of the growing season. Seasonal utilization can be collected at the end of a use period. This timing would indicate the amount of use at a particular time due to a certain stocking rate and mix of animals. It would also show the cumulative effect of grazing on plants through a sequence of growth stages.

Use patterns usually do not vary significantly from year to year unless there has been some modification in the number of days of use by animals, season of use, water locations, fences, or salt locations; unauthorized use; or unusual weather. It is not necessary to map a pasture or use area every year unless a management change or a significant change in the number of animals grazing in an area has occurred, e.g., a livestock adjustment or wild horse removal. Use pattern mapping is also essential for tracking the progress and impacts of range improvements and management changes.

V. METHODS

A. Browse Removal Methods

1. *Twig Length Measurement Method*
With the Twig Length Measurement Method, utilization is determined by measuring twigs on 25 to 50 browse plants after full annual growth has occurred and again after the period of use. The difference between the two measurements is an estimate of the amount of browse that has been utilized. Separate transects are run for different browse species. This method is used primarily on wildlife winter range.

a Areas of Use
This method of determining utilization is restricted to use on browse species that clearly exhibit annual twig growth, such as bitterbrush and mountain mahogany.

b Advantages and Limitations

(1) Percent utilization determined by measurement is more accurate than utilization determined by ocular observation. This method is useful in determining the amount of use made on browse plants by livestock and the amount of use made on the same browse plants by wildlife, wild horses, and/or wild burros. The degree of direct forage competition among different kinds of animals can be determined where there are discrete periods of use by different animals. Growth and use indexes can also be determined.

(2) Good utilization estimates can be obtained with this method even though twig volume is not uniformly distributed along the length of twigs. The results will vary with species due to twig growth characteristics.

(3) The method is not reliable on species that do not clearly exhibit annual twig growth, such as sagebrush and serviceberry. It is also not reliable in areas of the Southwest where annual twig growth may be masked by almost continuous growth or erratic seasonal growth after rains.

(4) The time and expense needed for gathering data are doubled because the measurements must be made twice a year.

c Equipment

- Study Location and Documentation Data form (see Appendix A)
- Twig Length Measurement form (see Illustration 1)
- Twenty-five to 50 numbered metal tags
- Roll of soft copper or aluminum wire
- 12-inch ruler or metric equivalent
- Compass
- Steel post
- Post driver

d **Training** This method does not require intensive training for field application. Examiners must be able to identify the plant species and recognize annual twig growth on the selected key species (see Section III.D.9).

e **Establishing Studies** Careful establishment of studies is a critical element in obtaining meaningful data. Select key species and determine the number, length, and location of the transects (see Section III.B.7).

(1) Collect data using several pilot transects to determine the number of transects needed and the number of observations to be made on each transect. These data are needed to determine if a statistically valid sample has been collected (see Section III.B.7).

(2) In mixed stands of key browse, such as bitterbrush and mountain mahogany, establish separate transects for each species.

(3) At the beginning of each study, determine the transect bearing and distance between observation points. Select a prominent distant landmark such as a large tree, rocky point, etc., that can be used as the transect bearing point.

(4) Plot the transects on detailed management unit maps and/or aerial photos (see beginning of Section III).

(5) Permanently mark the location of each study with a reference post and study location stake (see beginning of Section III).

(6) Number studies for proper identification to ensure that the data collected can be positively associated with specific studies on the ground (see Appendix B).

(7) Document the location and other pertinent information concerning the study on the Study Location and Documentation Data form (see beginning of Section III and Appendix A).

f **Sampling Process** After examiners are trained and are confident in their ability to recognize annual twig growth on the key species, proceed with the collection of utilization data.

(1) Tag plants of only one species per transect.

(2) Tag 25 to 50 plants of the selected key species on, each transect. Based on the analysis of past years' data, additional numbers of plants can be tagged to improve the precision of the estimate.

(3) Objectively tag plants along the transect. The first tagged plant should be a minimum of 10 paces from the beginning point of the transect along the transect bearing. The distance between tagged plants, thereafter, should depend on the length of the transect. Be sure to document the number of paces on the study location form.

(4) At the end of each pacing interval, select and tag the closest plant of the key species within a 180-degree zone ahead of the examiner. (See Appendix C for a schematic of the 180-degree selection zone.)

(5) Using soft copper or aluminum wire, attach a numbered metal tag to an individual branch that has a minimum of 10 twigs with new growth. The wire should be loosely attached on the branch to allow for future growth. Only one tag per plant is needed.

(6) Estimate the percent use that has already occurred and record on the Twig Length Measurement form (see Illustration 1).

(7) Measure the length of current growth (to the nearest 1/2 inch or nearest centimeter) on each twig from the point of tag attachment to the end of the branch. Record the data on the Twig Length Measurement form (see Illustration 1).

    (a) Make the first measurements after plants of the selected key species have attained full annual growth.

    (b) Make subsequent measurements after the period of use.

(8) Face the transect bearing point and begin the next pacing interval from the last tagged plant.

g Calculations Calculations can be made on the back of Twig Length Measurement form (see Illustration 1).

(1) Average estimated utilization prior to completion of full annual growth is the utilization that has occurred up to the time the first measurements are taken. Determine this utilization percentage by totaling the estimated percent utilization for the individual plants and dividing the total by the number of tagged plants.

$$\frac{\text{Total estimated \% utilization for the individual plants}}{\text{Number of tagged plants}} = \begin{array}{l}\text{Average estimated use} \\ \text{prior to completion} \\ \text{of full annual growth}\end{array}$$

(2) Percent utilization can be calculated as follows:

    (a) Total the twig measurements made after completion of full growth for each tagged plant.

    (b) Total the twig measurement made after the period of use for each tagged plant.

    (c) Calculate percent utilization of individual tagged plants as follows:

$$\frac{\begin{array}{l}\text{Total twig length by plant} \\ \text{after full annual growth}\end{array} - \begin{array}{l}\text{Total twig length by} \\ \text{plant after period of use}\end{array}}{\text{Total twig length by plants after full annual growth}} \times 100 = \text{Percent utilization}$$

(d) Calculate the average percent utilization for the key species on the transect by totaling the percent utilization for the individual tagged plants and dividing the total by the number of tagged plants. The average percent utilization may also be calculated as follows:

$$\frac{\text{Total twig length for all tagged plants after full annual growth} - \text{Total twig length for all plants after period of use}}{\text{Total twig length for all tagged plants after full annual growth}} \times 100 = \text{Measured percent utilization}$$

(e) Determine the total percent utilization by adding the average estimated utilization prior to completion of full annual growth and the average percent utilization for the period(s) of use.

$$\text{Average estimate used prior to completion of full annual growth} + \text{Measured percent utilization} = \text{Total percent}$$

(3) Growth index

(a) The growth index is the average twig length for all tagged plants as determined from the measurements obtained after completion of full annual growth. This index can be used to compare the amounts of growth that occur in different years and as an indication of species vigor.

(b) Calculate the growth index as follows:

$$\frac{\text{Total twig length for all tagged plants after full annual growth}}{\text{Number of twigs measured}} = \text{Growth index (Average twig length)}$$

(c) If use occurred on the plants prior to measurement after completion of full annual growth, adjust the growth index to account for this use as follows:

$$\frac{\text{Growth index (Average twig length)}}{100\% - \text{Average estimated use prior to completion of full annual growth}} \times 100 = \text{Adjusted growth index}$$

(5) Use index

(a) The use index is an indication of the volume of browse removed. This index can be used to compare the amounts of browse removed in different years.

(b) Calculate the use index by multiplying the total percent utilization times the adjusted growth index and dividing by 100. For example, if total utilization is 50 percent and the adjusted growth index is 6 inches, the use index is 3. If total utilization is 50 percent and the adjusted growth index is 3 inches, the use index is 1.5. Although utilization is the same in both examples, twice as much browse was removed in the first example.

$$\frac{\text{Total percent utilization} \times \text{Adjusted growth index}}{100} = \text{Use index}$$

h Data Analysis Data analysis consists of calculating confidence intervals around the average percent utilization estimate.

i References

Jensen, Charles H. and George W. Scotter. 1977. A comparison of twiglength and browsed-twig methods of determining browse utilization. J. Range Manage. 30:64-67.

Ferguson, Robert B. and Michael A. Marsden. 1977. Estimating overwinter bitterbrush utilization from twig diameter-length-weight relations. J. Range Manage. 30:231-236.

Smith, Arthur D. and Philip J. Urness. 1962. Analyses of the Twig Length Method of determining utilization of browse. Utah State Dept. of Fish & Game. Publication No. 62-9. 35p.

U.S. Department of Interior Bureau of Land Management. 1984. Rangeland Monitoring - Utilization Studies, TR4400-3.

Twig Length Measurement

Study Number	Examiner	Date	Kind and/or Class of Animal
Key Species	Allotment Name & Number	Pasture	Period of Use

Measurements after full annual growth
Nearest 1/2 inch ☐ Centimeter ☐

Tag No	1	2	3	4	5	6	7	8	9	10	11	12	Total Lngth	Est Use	No Twig Meas
Totals															

Measurements after period of use

1	2	3	4	5	6	7	8	9	10	11	12	Total Lngth	% Use by Plant
											Totals	

(Instructions for calculations on other side)

Notes (Use other side or another page, if necessary)

Illustration 1

Twig Length Measurement Method Form—Calculations:

1. Average estimated use prior to completion of full annual growth

$$\frac{\text{Total estimated \% utilization for the individual plants}}{\text{Number of tagged plants}} = \begin{array}{c}\text{Average estimated use} \\ \text{prior to completion} \\ \text{of full annual growth}\end{array} \qquad \underline{\hspace{2cm}} =$$

2. Percent utilization by individual plants

$$\frac{\begin{array}{c}\text{Total twig length by plant after full annual growth}\end{array} - \begin{array}{c}\text{Total twig length by plant after period of use}\end{array}}{\begin{array}{c}\text{Total twig length by plant after full annual growth}\end{array}} \times 100 = \begin{array}{c}\text{Percent} \\ \text{utilization}\end{array} \qquad \underline{\hspace{2cm}} \times 100 =$$

3. Total measured percent utilization

$$\frac{\begin{array}{c}\text{Total twig length for all tagged plants after full annual growth}\end{array} - \begin{array}{c}\text{Total twig length for all plants after period of use}\end{array}}{\begin{array}{c}\text{Total twig length for all tagged plants after full annual growth}\end{array}} \times 100 = \begin{array}{c}\text{Percent} \\ \text{utilization}\end{array} \qquad \underline{\hspace{2cm}} \times 100 =$$

4. Total percent utilization

$$\begin{array}{c}\text{Average estimate used prior to completion of full annual growth}\end{array} + \begin{array}{c}\text{Measured percent utilization}\end{array} = \text{Total percent} \qquad + \qquad =$$

5. Growth index

$$\frac{\begin{array}{c}\text{Total twig length for all tagged plants after full annual growth}\end{array}}{\text{Number of twigs measured}} = \text{Growth index (Average twig length)} \qquad \underline{\hspace{2cm}} =$$

6. Adjusted growth index

$$\frac{\text{Growth index (Average twig length)}}{\begin{array}{c}100\% - \text{Average estimated use prior to completion of full annual growth}\end{array}} \times 100 = \begin{array}{c}\text{Adjusted growth} \\ \text{index}\end{array} \qquad \underline{\hspace{2cm}} \times 100 =$$

7. Use index

$$\frac{\text{Total percent utilization} \times \text{Adjusted growth index}}{100} = \text{Use index} \qquad \frac{\underline{\hspace{0.5cm}} \times \underline{\hspace{0.5cm}}}{100} =$$

Illustration 1 *page 2* 31

Twig Length Measurement

Study Number	04N – 07W – 17 – 03
Date	9/1/95 11/30/96
Examiner	Jim Shoe
Kind and/or Class of Animal	Cattle
Key Species	PUTR 2
Allotment Name & Number	Chicken Creek 01573
Pasture	
Period of Use	8/1 to 11/30

Measurements after full annual growth — Nearest 1/2 inch ☐ Centimeter ☐

Tag No	1	2	3	4	5	6	7	8	9	10	11	12	Total Lngth	Est Use	No Twig Meas
1	5.5	5	6	7	6.5	6	7	5.5	6	6.5			61		10
2	7	5.5	6	6.5	7	6	6.5	5.5	7	5.5			62.5		10
3	6.5	6	6.5	5.5	6.5	5	6	4	5.5	6	5	6.5	69		12
4	6.5	7	6	6.5	5.5	5	6	5.5	4	3.5	2		57.5	5	11
5	5.5	6	6	6.5	5.5	6	7	4	6.5	5			58		10
6	7.5	6	5.5	6.5	7	6	6.5	3	5.5	6	5.5		65		11
7	5.5	7	7.5	6	7	6.5	6	6.5	3	5.5	3		60.5		10
8	4	6.5	5.5	6	6.5	4	3	4.5	5	6	3	1	55	5	12
9	6	4	4.5	5.5	5.5	5	5.5	6	4	7			53		10
10	6	5	6.5	4	3.5	7	6	6	6	3			53	5	10
11	6	5.5	8	6	6.5	5.5	7	4.5	6	6.5			61.5		10
12	5.5	3	7	7.5	5	6.5	4	6.5	5	4.5			54.5		10
13	7	7.5	6	8	5.5	7	4	5.5	6.5	7	6	5.5	75.5		12
Totals													786	15	138

Measurements after period of use

Tag No	1	2	3	4	5	6	7	8	9	10	11	12	Total Lngth	% Use by Plant
1	5.5	5	6	7	6	5	5	2	4	2			47.5	22
2	7	5.5	6	6.5	7	6	6.5	4	5	4			57.5	8
3	6.5	6	6.5	5.5	5	4	5	4	4.5	4.5	4	4	60.5	12
4	6.5	7	6	6.5	4.5	4	6	5	3.5	2	1		52	10
5	5.5	6	6	6.5	5.5	4	3	4	3.5	2			46	21
6	7.5	6	5.5	6.5	7	6	6.5	3	4	3.5	5		60.5	7
7	5.5	7	7.5	6	7	6.5	6	6.5	3	5.5			60.5	0
8	4	6.5	5.5	6	6.5	4	3	4.5	4	4	2	.5	50.5	8
9	6	4	4.5	5.5	3.5	5	5.5	6	4	5.5			51.5	3
10	6	5	6.5	4	6.5	7	6	3	2	2			45	15
11	6	5.5	8	6	6.5	5.5	7	4	3.5	4			56	9
12	5.5	3	7	7.5	5	6.5	4	6.5	5	4.5			54.5	0
13	7	7.5	6	8	5.5	7	4	5.5	6.5	5.5	6	4	72.5	4
Totals													714.5	119

(Instructions for calculations on other side)

Notes (Use other side or another page, if necessary)

32

Illustration 1

Twig Length Measurement Method Form—Calculations:

1. Average estimated use prior to completion of full annual growth

$$\frac{\text{Total estimated \% utilization for the individual plants}}{\text{Number of tagged plants}} = \begin{array}{c}\text{Average estimated use}\\ \text{prior to completion}\\ \text{of full annual growth}\end{array} \qquad \frac{15}{13} = 1\%$$

2. Percent utilization by individual plants

$$\frac{\begin{array}{c}\text{Total twig length by plant after full annual growth}\end{array} - \begin{array}{c}\text{Total twig length by plant after period of use}\end{array}}{\begin{array}{c}\text{Total twig length by plant after full annual growth}\end{array}} \times 100 = \begin{array}{c}\text{Percent}\\\text{utilization}\end{array} \quad \frac{61 - 47.5}{60} \times 100 = 22\%$$

3. Total measured percent utilization

$$\frac{\begin{array}{c}\text{Total twig length for all tagged plants after full annual growth}\end{array} - \begin{array}{c}\text{Total twig length for all plants after period of use}\end{array}}{\begin{array}{c}\text{Total twig length for all tagged plants after full annual growth}\end{array}} \times 100 = \begin{array}{c}\text{Percent}\\\text{utilization}\end{array} \quad \frac{786 - 714.5}{786} \times 100 = 9\%$$

4. Total percent utilization

$$\begin{array}{c}\text{Average estimate}\\ \text{used prior to completion of}\\ \text{full annual growth}\end{array} + \begin{array}{c}\text{Measured}\\ \text{percent utilization}\end{array} = \text{Total percent} \quad 1 + 9 = 10\%$$

5. Growth index

$$\frac{\begin{array}{c}\text{Total twig length for all tagged plants after full annual growth}\end{array}}{\text{Number of twigs measured}} = \text{Growth index (Average twig length)} \quad \frac{786}{138} = 5.7 \text{ inches}$$

6. Adjusted growth index

$$\frac{\text{Growth index (Average twig length)}}{100\% - \begin{array}{c}\text{Average estimate use prior to completion of full annual growth}\end{array}} \times 100 = \begin{array}{c}\text{Adjusted growth}\\\text{index}\end{array} \quad \frac{5.7}{100 - 1} \times 100 = 5.8 \text{ inches}$$

7. Use index

$$\frac{\text{Total percent utilization} \times \text{Adjusted growth index}}{100} = \text{Use index} \quad \frac{10 \times 58}{100} = .6$$

Illustration 1 *page 2* 33

2. *Cole Browse Method* The Cole Browse Method is used to collect utilization data on browse species. This method provides data on age and form class, availability and hedging, estimated utilization, and growth and use indexes for the browse component of the plant community. These data are used to make annual utilization and trend estimates. Separate transects are run for different browse species.

a **Areas of Use** This method can be used in a wide variety of vegetation types where browse key species clearly exhibit annual leader growth.

b **Advantages and Limitations** The Cole Browse Method is more rapid than methods that require measurements; however, it is somewhat less accurate because estimates rather than measurements are used to determine utilization. There can be considerable variation in utilization estimates as well as in age and form class estimates among examiners. Plant growth characteristics, weather conditions, and site conditions may have an equal or greater influence on the appearance of plants than leader use. In addition, age class and form class may not always be sensitive indicators of the effects of browsing.

c **Equipment**

- Study Location and Documentation Data form (see Appendix A)
- Cole Browse form (see Illustration 2)
- Compass
- 10-foot tape
- Steel posts
- Post driver
- 12-inch ruler or metric equivalent

d **Training** The accuracy of utilization percentage estimates depends on the thoroughness of training. Examiners should be trained to identify browse species and to recognize annual leader growth, availability of browse, percent utilization, degree of hedging, and age class of browse plants (see Section III.D.9).

e **Establishing Studies** Careful establishment of studies is a critical element in obtaining meaningful data. Select key species and determine the number, length, and location of the transects (see Section III.B.7).

(1) Collect data using several pilot transects to determine the number of transects needed and the number of observations to be made on each transect. These data are needed to determine if a statistically valid sample has been collected (see Section III.B.7).

(2) At the beginning of each study, determine the transect bearing and distance between observation points. Select a prominent distant landmark such as a large tree, rocky point, etc., that can be used as the transect bearing point.

(3) Plot the transects on detailed management unit maps and/or aerial photos (see beginning of Section III).

(4) Permanently mark the location of each study with a reference post and study location stake (see beginning of Section III).

(5) Number studies for proper identification to ensure that the data collected can be positively associated with specific studies on the ground (see Appendix B).

(6) Document the location and other pertinent information concerning the study on the Study Location and Documentation Data form (see beginning of Section III and Appendix A).

(7) Temporary transects may be used for locating study sites or for gathering data on browse stands outside study sites. These transects do not need to be marked on the ground.

f Sampling Process Collect data beginning with the first selected plant; make the necessary observations, estimates, and measurements; and then record the data on the Cole Browse form (see Illustration 2).

(1) Sample only one species on each transect.

(2) *Form class* Observe the selected plant and check the appropriate Form Class column on the form.

(a) The form classes are as follows:

No.	Form Class
1	All available, little or no hedging
2	All available, moderately hedged
3	All available, severely hedged
4	Partially available, little or no hedging
5	Partially available, moderately hedged
6	Partially available, severely hedged
7	Unavailable
8	Dead

(b) Availability refers to browse available to the animals.

(c) The three degrees of hedging are based on the length and appearance of two-year-old wood (previous year's leaders) immediately below the current leaders (see Appendix D). If more than one degree of hedging is evident on a plant, form class is based on the predominant or average condition. The three degrees of hedging are:

Little or no hedging - Two-year-old wood is relatively long and unaltered or only slightly altered.

Moderately hedged - Two-year-old wood is fairly long but most of it has been altered from the normal growth form.

Severely hedged - Two-year-old wood is relatively short and/or strongly altered from the normal growth form.

(d) Browse plants are considered to reflect the normal growth form when less than 50 percent of the two-year-old growth (the previous year's leaders) has clipped ends and most of the current leaders extend directly from terminal buds off two-year-old wood. Alterations from the normal growth form are reflected when 50 percent or more of the two-year-old wood has clipped ends. Current leaders occur mostly as extensions from lateral buds off two-year-old wood in the moderately hedged condition or as clumped lateral and/or adventitious sprouts in severely hedged condition.

(e) The length of two-year-old wood reflects the relative vigor of the previous year's leader growth and/or the effects of prior use. Since the degrees of hedging are confined to two-year-old wood, they reflect the effects of use during a previous year, or a succession of previous years.

(f) The three degrees of hedging provide a measure of the relative condition of browse plants and help in assessing the short-term effects of different intensities of leader use.

(3) *Age class* Age class data reflect the establishment, survival, and decadence of key browse plants. Observe the selected plant and check the appropriate Age Class Column on the form. An age class designation is not made for plants in form classes 7 and 8. The four age classes are:

S - Seedling - New plants that have survived at least one growing season, but are not more than 2 or 3 years old. The basal stems are generally 1/8 inch or less in diameter.

Y - Young - Young plants usually less than 10 years old. They have an elongated growth form and simple branching with basal stems no greater than approximately .5 inch in diameter.

M - Mature - Plants more than 10 years old. They are distinguished by heavier, often gnarled stems, and complex branching. Canopy is made up of more than 50 percent living wood. Basal stems are often greater than .5 inch in diameter.

D - Decadent - Browse plants with more than 50 percent of the canopy area dead.

(4) *Leader use estimates* Leader use is an estimate of the intensity of use on browse plants available to the animals. Estimate the percent of available leaders that have been browsed on each sample plant. This estimate is based on the number of leaders that have been browsed and not on the percent of growth removed. Leader use estimates are not made for plants in form classes 7 and 8. Determine the use class that the estimate falls in and enter the class value in the Leader Use Column on the form. For example, if estimated leader use is 15 percent, then the recorded value will be 25 percent; if estimated use is 80 percent, the recorded value will be 75 percent. The leader use class percentage ranges and the corresponding class values are:

Leader Use Class Percentage Range	Class Values
0	0
1-10	5
11-40	25
41-60	50
61-90	75
91-100	95

(5) ***Leader length measurements*** Measure current growth on each ungrazed leader on the available portion of each sampled plant on the transect. These measurements are taken to determine the average annual growth or growth index. Record these measurements (to the nearest .5 inch or nearest centimeter) on the back of the form.

(6) ***Selecting the nearest plant*** To select the next plant to be sampled, face toward the transect bearing point, pace the specified distance, and then select and sample the nearest plant of the key species that occurs within a 180-degree zone (see Appendix C). Repeat this routine until the desired number of plants have been sampled. To lengthen a transect, increase the distance between observations (10 paces, 20 paces, etc.). At the end of the pacing interval, select the nearest plant in the 180-degree zone. Use the same pacing interval throughout the transect.

g Calculations Make the calculations and record the results in the appropriate column or blank on the Cole Browse form (see Illustration 2).

(1) ***Form class summary*** Total the number of plants in each form class and enter the value in the Total Column on the form. Calculate the percent composition by form class as follows:

$$\frac{\text{Total no. of plants in a form class}}{\text{Total no. of plants sampled}} \times 100 = \text{Percent composition by form class}$$

Enter the value in the Percent Column on the form.

(2) ***Age class summary*** Total the number of plants in each age class and enter the value in the Total Column on the form. Calculate percent composition by age class as follows:

$$\frac{\text{Total no. of plants in an age class}}{\text{Total no. of plants sampled}} \times 100 = \text{Percent composition by age class}$$

Enter the value in the Percent Column on the form.

(3) *Average leader use* Calculate the average leader use, being sure to exclude the number of plants that are dead or unavailable from the total number of plants sampled:

$$\frac{\text{Total estimated leader use for all plants}}{\text{Total no. of plants sampled}} = \text{Average leader use (\%)}$$

Record the value on the form.

(4) *Average leader length or growth index*

    (a) The growth index is the average length of the ungrazed leaders on the sampled plants. This index can be used to compare the amounts of growth which occur in different years and as an indication of species vigor.

    (b) Calculate the average leader length or growth index as follows:

$$\frac{\text{Total length of ungrazed leaders}}{\text{total no. of leaders measured}} = \begin{array}{l}\text{Average length of}\\ \text{ungrazed leaders or growth index}\end{array}$$

    Record the value on the form.

(5) *Use index*

    (a) The use index is an indication of the volume of browse removed. This index can be used to compare amounts of browse removed in different years.

    (b) Calculate the use index by multiplying the average leader use (%) times the average leader length (growth index) and dividing by 100. Record the use index on the form. For example, if average leader use is 50 percent and the average leader length is 6 inches, the use index is 3. If average leader use is 50 percent and the average leader length is 3 inches, the use index is 1.5. Although utilization is the same in both examples, twice as much browse was removed in the first example.

$$\frac{\text{Average leader use \% x Growth index}}{100} = \text{Use index}$$

h Data Analysis Confidence intervals can be constructed around median or average leader use percentages. The number of individuals in different form and age classes can be compared to desired or expected values using Chi Square analysis.

i References

U.S. Department of Interior Bureau of Land Management. 1984. Rangeland Monitoring - Utilization Studies, TR4400-3.

Cole Browse

Study Number	Date	Examiner

Allotment Name & Number	Pasture

Key Species	Kind and/or Class of Animal	Period of Use

Pl No	Form Class								Age Class				Leader Use -%	Pl No	Form Class								Age Class				Leader Use -%
	1	2	3	4	5	6	7	8	S	Y	M	D			1	2	3	4	5	6	7	8	S	Y	M	D	
1														26													
2														27													
3														28													
4														29													
5														30													
6														31													
7														32													
8														33													
9														34													
10														35													
11														36													
12														37													
13														38													
14														39													
15														40													
16														41													
17														42													
18														43													
19														44													
20														45													
21														46													
22														47													
23														48													
24														49													
25														50													

Tot. % Form Classes

____ ____ 1 - All available, Little or no hedging
____ ____ 2 - All available, Moderately hedged
____ ____ 3 - All available, Severely Hedged
____ ____ 4 - Partially available, Little or no hedging
____ ____ 5 - Partially available, Moderately hedged
____ ____ 6 - Partially available, Severely Hedged
            Subtotal

____ ____ 7 - Unavailable
____ ____ 8 - Dead
            Total

Average Leader Length		Use Index	

Tot. % Age Classes   Total ____

____ ____ S - Seedling, < 1/8" diam.
____ ____ Y - Young, 1/8" to 1/2" diam.
____ ____ M - Mature, > 1/2" diam.
____ ____ D - Decadent, 50% or more dead
____ ____ Total

Leader Use Class	Value	Average Leader Use
0%	0%	
1-10%	5%	
11-40%	25%	
41-60%	50%	
61-90%	75%	____
91-100%	95%	

Illustration 2   39

Pl No	Leader Length										Total Length	No Ldrs. Meas.	Notes (use another page, if necessary)
	1	2	3	4	5	6	7	8	9	10			Page 2
1													
2													
3													
4													
5													
6													
7													
8													
9													
10													
11													
12													
13													
14													
15													
16													
17													
18													
19													
20													
21													
22													
23													
24													
25													
26													
27													
28													
29													
30													
31													
32													
33													
34													
35													
36													
37													
38													
39													
40													
41													
42													
43													
44													
45													
46													
47													
48													
49													
50													
										Totals			

Total Length / No Leaders Meas. = Average Leader Length

_____ =

Illustration 2 *page 2*

Cole Browse

Study Number	Date	Examiner
13 S - 27 E - 11 - 05	2/28/96	Suzie Clump

Allotment Name & Number	Pasture
Purple Ridge 11234	Mahogany

Key Species	Kind and/or Class of Animal	Period of Use
CEMO 2	Cattle	11/1 to 2/28

PI No	Form Class 1	2	3	4	5	6	7	8	Age Class S	Y	M	D	Leader Use -%	PI No	Form Class 1	2	3	4	5	6	7	8	Age Class S	Y	M	D	Leader Use -%
1		X									X		50	26	X									X			5
2				X							X		5	27	X									X			5
3	X									X			25	28	X									X			25
4		X									X		25	29	X									X			50
5		X									X		25	30	X								X				25
6				X							X		50	31													
7				X							X		25	32													
8					X						X		75	33													
9						X							—	34													
10	X									X			25	35													
11	X									X			25	36													
12					X								—	37													
13				X							X		5	38													
14	X								X				5	39													
15	X								X				25	40													
16							X						—	41													
17		X								X			50	42													
18	X										X		25	43													
19	X										X		25	44													
20		X										X	50	45													
21				X							X		25	46													
22				X							X		5	47													
23							X						—	48													
24	X									X			25	49													
25		X										X	25	50													

Total **705**

Tot. % Form Classes

13	43	1 - All available, Little or no hedging
6	20	2 - All available, Moderately hedged
0	—	3 - All available, Severely Hedged
4	13	4 - Partially available, Little or no hedging
2	7	5 - Partially available, Moderately hedged
1	3	6 - Partially available, Severely Hedged
26	86	Subtotal
2	7	7 - Unavailable
2	7	8 - Dead
30	100	Total

Tot. % Age Classes

3	12	S - Seedling, < 1/8" diam.
9	35	Y - Young, 1/8" to 1/2" diam.
12	46	M - Mature, > 1/2" diam.
2	7	D - Decadent, 50% or more dead
26	100	Total

Leader Use Class	Value	Average
0%	0%	Leader Use
1-10%	5%	
11-40%	25%	
41-60%	50%	27%
61-90%	75%	
91-100%	95%	

Average Leader Length	7 inches	Use Index	1.9

Illustration 2   41

Pl No	Leader Length 1	2	3	4	5	6	7	8	9	10	Total Length	No Ldrs. Meas.
1	7	6.5	8	6.5	3	6					37	6
2	8	6	7.5	6.5	5	7	6	6.5			52.5	8
3	6.5	7	8	5	7.5	7	8	5.5	6	7.5	68	10
4	8	6.5	7	7	7	7.5	6.5	7	6	6	68.5	10
5	7.5	8	6	7	7	6.5	5	7.5	7		61.5	9
6	7.5	7	8	6.5	9						38	5
7	7	9	8.5	7	8	6.5	7				53	7
8	6	7.5	7								20.5	3
9												—
10	5.5	7.5	6	8	8.5	7	9	7			58.5	8
11	7.5	8	6	9	5.5	6	8	8	8		66	9
12												—
13	7.5	9	9	6.5	7	8	6	7	9	7	76	10
14	6.5	6	7	7	6.5	5					38	6
15	6.5	7	8	5	7						33.5	5
16												—
17	5.5	8	7	6.5							27	4
18	8	7	8	8	6.5	4	7.5	7	7	7	70	10
19	9	8.5	8.5	6	7	6.5	5	7	6	6	69.5	10
20	8	8.5	7	6							29.5	4
21	7	9	7.5	8	6	5.5	7				50	7
22	7	8.5	6	6.5	7	6.5	6	6	6		59.5	9
23												—
24	7	6.5	5	4.5	7	9	9	8	7	8	71	10
25	8.5	9	7.5	7	7	7	8	8.5	6		68.5	9
26	8.5	6.5	9	8.5	5	9	6.5	8	8	8	77	10
27	6.5	7	9	8.5	7	7	7.5	7	4	8	71.5	10
28	5	7.5	8	8	8	7	7.5	6	9		66	9
29	9	9	8.5	7	7	8					48.5	6
30	8	6	6.5	6	6.5	8	7	7			55	8
31												
32												
33												
34												
35												
36												
37												
38												
39												
40												
41												
42												
43												
44												
45												
46												
47												
48												
49												
50												
										Totals	1434	202

Notes (use another page, if necessary)

$$\frac{\text{Total Length}}{\text{No Leaders Meas.}} = \text{Average Leader Length} \quad \frac{1434}{202} = 7 \text{ inches}$$

3. *Extensive Browse Method* With the Extensive Browse Method, pace transects are run to collect vegetation data. This method provides data on utilization, species composition, age class, form classes, availability, and hedging for the browse component of the plant community.

a **Areas of Use** This method can be used within a wide variety of vegetation types.

b **Advantages and Limitations** The Extensive Browse Method is rapid and can be used on all browse species. It is well adapted to situations where browse data must be obtained from large areas with limited personnel. All browse species within the plant community can be sampled on one transect. The method is more rapid than methods which require measurements. However, it is somewhat less accurate than measurement methods in determining utilization because estimates rather than measurements are used. This method is designed to eliminate personal bias and maximize consistency.

c **Equipment**

(1) Study Location and Documentation Data form (see Appendix A)

(2) Extensive Browse form (see Illustration 3)

(3) Tally counter (optional)

d **Training** The accuracy of utilization percentage estimates depends upon the thoroughness of training. Examiners should be trained to identify browse species and to recognize annual leader growth, availability of browse, percent utilization, degree of hedging, and age class of browse plants (see Section III.D.9).

e **Establishing Studies** Careful establishment of studies is a critical element in obtaining meaningful data. Select key species and determine the number, length, and location of the transects (see Section III.B.7).

(1) Collect data using several pilot transects to determine the number of transects needed and the number of observations to be made on each transect. These data are needed to determine if a statistically valid sample has been collected (see Section III.B.7).

(2) At the beginning of each study, determine the transect bearing and distance between observation points. Select a prominent distant landmark such as a large tree, rocky point, etc., that can be used as the transect bearing point.

(3) Plot the transects on detailed management unit maps and/or aerial photos (see beginning of Section III).

(4) Although transects are not permanent, plot them on detailed management unit maps and/or aerial photos for documentation and future reference.

(5) Number studies for proper identification to ensure that the data collected can be positively associated with specific studies on the ground (see Appendix B).

(6) Record important information about the transect and any special resource conditions under "Notes" Extensive Browse form, or on the Study Location and Documentation Data form (see Illustration 3 and Appendix A)

(7) Locate the "heaviest used" or "representative" areas in a management unit. The intent is to find several areas used intensively during the period of use. These may occur in the same general location each year, but will probably fluctuate. Transects are located in heavy use areas since vegetation changes which occur as a result of browsing will be evident first on these areas.

f Sampling Process After examiners are trained and are confident in their ability to recognize the availability of browse, degree of utilization, degree of hedging, and age classes of browse plants, proceed with the collection of data.

(1) *Selecting the sample plants*

(a) At the end of each pacing interval, face toward the transect bearing point and then select and sample the nearest browse plant that occurs within a 180-degree zone. (See Appendix C for a schematic of the 180-degree selection zone.)

(b) Begin each pacing interval from the last sampled plant. Pace toward the transect bearing point in the interspaces between browse plants. It is not necessary to pace in an absolutely straight line.

(2) *Collecting data* Record utilization estimates as well as the form class and age class on the selected browse plant by species on the Extensive Browse form (see Illustration 3). Use a dot count or tally counter to keep track of the number of plants sampled.

(a) *Utilization* Select a branch and estimate the amount of utilization of current annual growth.

- *Select a branch at random. For example:*

  Note the second-hand location or the digital seconds readout on a watch.

  Using the route of travel along the transect line as the 6 o'clock - 12 o'clock line, go to the position on the browse plant that is indicated by the location of the second hand or the digital second readout. (Example - 20 seconds represents the 4 o'clock position.)

- *Select an available branch on that side of the plant.*

  Select ten leaders of annual growth and determine the number of these leaders that show any evidence of use. Convert this number to percent (i.e., two leaders used equals 20 percent use, six leaders used equals 60 percent use, etc). Record the value by dot tally in the appropriate column on the form.

After sampling a total of 50 plants, figure the average utilization for each species encountered on the first half of the transect. Circle the plant code for all species averaging 50 percent or greater use (see Section V.A.3.g).

- *Sample points 51-100 as follows:*

If the selected plants are one of the circled species, record utilization estimates as well as the form class and age class in the same manner as for the first 50 plants.

If the next selected plants are not one of the circled species, record utilization estimates as well as the form class and age class. In addition, locate the nearest plant of any of the circled species and record its utilization (only) in the appropriate column opposite the species plant code. Do not record age class and form class for these additional plants.

(b) *Age class* Age class data reflect the establishment, survival, and decadence of key browse plants. Observe the selected plant and record (by dot tally) the age class by species in the appropriate column on the form. The four age classes are as follows:

S - Seedling - New plants that have survived at least one growing season, but are not more than 2 or 3 years old. The basal stems are generally 1/8 inch or less in diameter.

Y - Young - Young plants usually less than 10 years old. They have an elongated growth form and simple branching with basal stems no greater than approximately .5 inch in diameter.

M - Mature - Plants more than 10 years old. They are distinguished by heavier, often gnarled stems, and complex branching. Canopy is made up of more than 50 percent living wood. Basal stems are often greater than .5 inch in diameter.

D - Decadent - Browse plants with more than 50 percent of the canopy area dead.

(c) *Form class* Observe the selected plant and record (by dot tally) the form class by species in the appropriate column on the form.

- *The form classes are as follows:*

No.	Form Class
1	All available, little or no hedging
2	All available, moderately hedged
3	All available, severely hedged
4	Partially available, little or no hedging
5	Partially available, moderately hedged
6	Partially available, severely hedged
7	Unavailable
8	Dead

- Availability refers to browse available to the animals.

- The three degrees of hedging are based on the length and appearance of two-year-old wood (previous year's leaders) immediately below the current leaders (see Appendix D). If more than one degree of hedging is evident on a plant, form class is based on the predominant or average condition. *The three degrees of hedging are:*

Little or no hedging - Two-year-old wood is relatively long and unaltered or only slightly altered.

Moderately hedged - Two-year-old wood is fairly long but most of it has been altered from the normal growth form.

Severely hedged - Two-year-old wood is relatively short and/or strongly altered from the normal growth form.

- Browse plants are considered to reflect the normal growth form when less than 50 percent of the two-year-old growth (the previous year's leaders) has clipped ends and a most of the current leaders extend directly from terminal buds off two-year-old wood. Alterations from the normal growth form are reflected when 50 percent or more of the two-year-old wood has clipped ends. Current leaders occur mostly as extensions from lateral buds off two-year-old wood in the moderately hedged condition or as clumped lateral and/or adventitious sprouts in the severely hedged condition.

- The length of two-year-old wood reflects the relative vigor of the previous year's leader growth and/or the effects of prior use. Since the degrees of hedging are confined to two-year-old wood, they reflect the effects of use during a previous year, or a succession of previous years.

- The three degrees of hedging provide a measure of the relative condition of browse plants and help in assessing the short-term effects of different intensities of leader use.

g Calculations Make the calculations and record the results in the appropriate columns on the Extensive Browse form (see Illustration 3).

(1) *Average utilization by species*

(a) For each species, multiply the number of browse plants tallied in each percentage block by the percent indicated in the column heading (0, 10, 20, 30, etc.). Add the figures from each block and enter the total in the Total Percent Utilized Column on the form.

(b) Add the dot tallies for each browse species to determine the total number of plants sampled of that species and enter the total in the Number of Plants Column on the form.

(c) Calculate the average percent utilization for each species by dividing the total percent utilized by the total number of plants. Enter the value in the Average Percent Utilization Column on the form.

(2) *Age class summary* Add the dot tallies for each age class and enter the totals in the Total Number of Plants Row on the form. Because the age class is determined for 100 plants on the transect, these totals represent the percent composition by age class for the browse portion of the plant community.

(3) *Form class summary* Add the dot tallies for each form class and enter the totals in the Total Number of Plants Row on the form. Because the form class is determined for 100 plants on the transect, these totals represent the percent composition by form class for the browse portion of the plant community.

(4) *Percent composition by species* Add the form class dot tallies for each browse species and enter the total in the Number of Plants Column on the form. Because the form class is determined for 100 plants on the transect, these totals represent the species composition percentages for the browse portion of the plant community.

h Data Analysis Confidence intervals are calculated for average utilization percentages. The number of individuals in different form and age classes can be compared to desired or expected values using Chi Square analysis.

i References

Hooper, Jack F. and Harold F. Heady. 1970. An economic analysis of optimum rates of grazing in the California annual-type grassland. J. Range Manage. 23:307-311.

U.S. Department of Interior Bureau of Land Management. 1984. Rangeland Monitoring - Utilization Studies, TR4400-3.

Extensive Browse

Study Number		Date	Examiner

Allotment Name & Number	Pasture

Kind and/or Class of Animal	Period of Use

Species	Percent Utilization											Total % Utilized	Number of Plants	Average % Utilized
	0	10	20	30	40	50	60	70	80	90	100			

Species	Age Class				Form Class								No Plnt (and % Comp)
	S	Y	M	D	1	2	3	4	5	6	7	8	
Tot. no. Plants (and % comp)													

Notes (use other side or another page, if necessary)   (Instructions for calculations on other side)

Illustration 3

Calculating Average Utilization by Species

1. For each species, multiply the number of browse plants tallied in each percentage block by the percent indicated in the column heading (0, 10, 20, 30, etc.). Add the figures from each block to determine the total percent utilized.

2. Add the dot tallies for each browse species to determine the total number of plants sampled of that species.

3. Calculate the average percent utilization for each species by dividing the total percent utilization by the total number of plants.

Age Class Summary Calculations

Add the dot tallies for each age class. Because the age class is determined for 100 plants on the transect, these totals represent the percent composition by age class for the browse portion of the plant community.

From Class Summary Calculations

Add the dot tallies for each form class. Because the form class is determined for 100 plants on the transect, these totals represent the percent composition by form class for the browse portion of the plant community.

Calculating Composition By Species

Add the form class dot tallies for each browse species. Because the form class is determined for 100 plants on the transect, the totals represent the species composition percentages for the browse portion of the plant community.

Illustration 3 *page 2*

49

Extensive Browse

Study Number	Date	Examiner
27N - 01E - 19 - 01	3/28/96	S. Clump

Allotment Name & Number	Pasture
Window Rock 12139	Rock

Kind and/or Class of Animal	Period of Use
Sheep	1/15 to 3/31

Species	Percent Utilization											Total % Utilized	Number of Plants	Average % Utilized
	0	10	20	30	40	50	60	70	80	90	100			
(PUTR 2)				∴	⊠	⊠⊠⊓	⊠∷	⊡∵	•			3110	60	52
CEMO 2		⊠•	⊠⊡	⊡	⊓∴		:					1030	44	23
CHVI 8	⊓∴	⊠•	∷	:		•						280	23	12
ARTRV	∴	⊠		•								130	14	9

Species	Age Class				Form Class								No Plnt (and % Comp)
	S	Y	M	D	1	2	3	4	5	6	7	8	
PUTR 2	•	∴	⊠∴	:	⊠	⊓∴	:	•	•				19
CEMO 2	∷	⊠:	⊠⊠⊓	•	⊠⊠⊠	∷		⊓∴	:	:			44
CHVI 8		⊓	⊠⊓∴		⊠⊠	:		:					23
ARTRV		∴	⊠•		⊠∷								14
Tot. no. Plants (and % comp)	5	26	66	4	72	12	2	9	3	2			

Notes (use other side or another page, if necessary)   (Instructions for calculations on other side)

Illustration 3

B. Residue Measuring Methods

1. Stubble Height Method The concept of this method is to measure stubble height, or height (in centimeters or inches) of herbage left ungrazed at any given time. This method, because of its simple application, is becoming a well-accepted method for expressing rangeland use.

This method would be used after stubble height standards for specific plant communities had been developed. As an example, a stubble height of 4 inches might be specified to provide streambank protection, to trap sediments, and to rebuild degraded stream channels in riparian areas.

a Areas of Use Stubble height standards and measurements have been used primarily in riparian areas; however, this method may also be used for upland sites. Adequate stubble height on streamside areas is needed at the end of the growing season for maintenance of plant vigor and streambank protection.

b Advantages and Disadvantages Stubble height measurements are simple, quick, and accurate. This method can be used to monitor large areas in less time than is needed with traditional utilization study methods. Statistical reliability improves because numerous measurements can be taken in a relatively short time. Limitations of the method may stem from infrequent application in a variety of rangeland ecosystems. While stubble height has been used with great success in riparian areas, there needs to be more research in a variety of other plant communities.

c Equipment

- Study Location and Documentation Data form (see Appendix A)
- Stubble Height form (see Illustration 4)
- Tape measure

d Training Minimal training of examiners is needed to use this method. Examiners must be able to identify the plant species. This method requires measuring stubble heights of selected key species, which can easily be accomplished by agency personnel, permittees, or other interested individuals.

e Establishing Studies Careful establishment of studies is a critical element in obtaining meaningful data. Select key species and determine the number, length, and location of the transects (see Section III.B.7). Document the location and other pertinent information concerning transects on the Stubble Height form.

(1) Collect data using several pilot transects to determine the number of transects needed and the number of observations to be made on each transect. These data are needed to determine if a statistically valid sample has been collected (see Section III.B.7).

(2) At the beginning of each study, determine the transect bearing and distance between observation points. Select a prominent distant landmark such as a large tree, rocky point, etc., that can be used as the transect bearing point.

(3) Plot the transects on detailed management unit maps and/or aerial photos (see beginning of Section III).

(4) Permanently mark the location of each study with a reference post and study location stake (see beginning of Section III).

(5) Number studies for proper identification to ensure that the data collected can be positively associated with specific studies on the ground (see Appendix B).

(6) Document the location and other pertinent information concerning the study on the Study Location and Documentation Data form (see beginning of Section III and Appendix A).

f Sampling Process At specified intervals, measure the stubble height of the key species nearest to the toe of the right foot and record on the Stubble Height form (Illustration 4). Measurements should be in inches or centimeters of leaf stubble left. For riparian sites, sampling should be done along both sides of a stream segment. For upland sites and wet meadow riparian sites, measurements should be taken along a predetermined course or transect. In either situation, stubble height data can be collected using the linear or baseline techniques described in Section III.A.2.

g Calculations Use data from the Stubble Height form for calculating the average stubble height by species.

h Data Analysis Confidence levels should be calculated for the median. See Technical Reference, *Measuring & Monitoring Plant Populations*, for information on determining confidence intervals.

i References

Anderson, E. William and Wilbur F. Currier. 1973. Evaluating zones of utilization. J. Range Manage. 26:87-91.

Gierisch, Ralph K. 1967. An adaptation of the grazed plant method for estimating utilization of Thurber fescue. J. Range Manage. 20:108-111.

Lommasson, T. and Chandler Jensen. 1938. Grass volume tables for determining range utilization. Science 87:444.

———— 1943. Determining utilization of range grasses from height-weight tables. J. Forestry 41:589-593.

McDougald, Neil K. and Richard C. Platt. 1976. A method of determining utilization for wet mountain meadows on the summit allotment, Sequoia National Forest, California. J. Range Manage. 29:497-501.

Reid, E.H. and G.D. Pickford. 1941. A comparison of the ocular-estimate by-plot and the stubble-height methods for determining percentage utilization of range grasses. J. Forestry 39:935-941.

Stubble Height

Study Number				Date	Examiner	
Allotment Name & Number				Pasture		

	1	2	3	4	5	6
Site (or)						
Species						
1						
2						
3						
4						
5						
6						
7						
8						
9						
10						
11						
12						
13						
14						
15						
16						
17						
18						
19						
20						
21						
22						
23						
24						
25						
26						
27						
28						
29						
30						
31						
32						
33						
34						
35						
36						
Total						
Average						

(Record averages on back of form.)

Illustration 4

Stubble Height Summary

Species	Total Stubble Height	Number of Plants	Average Stubble Height
Totals			

Notes:

Stubble Height

Study Number			Date		Examiner	
HDQ 1			8/3/95		MJB	

Allotment Name & Number				Pasture		
East Fork 46045				Willow Spring		

	1	2	3	4	5	6
Site (or) Species	HIMU 2	BOER 4	BOCU			
1	4	3	2			
2	7	5				
3	6	6	4			
4	8	4				
5	2	2	4			
6	5	1	4			
7	3	7				
8	6	4				
9	9		3			
10	4	3	5			
11	4	5	3			
12	3	6	6			
13	2					
14	5	2	4			
15	4	4	5			
16	2	4				
17	3					
18	6	6	2			
19	2	6				
20	7					
21	4	3	4			
22	5					
23	3	4				
24	6	3	4			
25	5	3	4			
26	3					
27	6	5	3			
28	6	7				
29	2	6				
30	5	4	2			
31	3					
32	5	2				
33	6	4	2			
34	4		2			
35	4	3				
36	5					
Total	165	112	63			
Average	4.6	4.1	3.5			

(Record averages on back of form.)

Illustration 4

Stubble Height Summary

Species	Total Stubble Height	Number of Plants	Average Stubble Height
HiMU 2	165	36	4.6
BOER	112	27	4.1
BOCU	63	18	3.5
Totals	340	81	4.2

Notes:

2. *Visual Obstruction Method - Robel Pole* This method can be used to determine the amount of standing biomass remaining on an area after a use period. It is commonly referred to as the Robel Pole Method.

a **Areas of Use** The Visual Obstruction Method is effective in both upland and riparian areas where vegetation is less than 4 feet tall.

b **Advantages and Disadvantages** The Visual Obstruction measurements are simple, quick, and accurate. This method can be used to monitor height and vertical density of standing vegetation over large areas quickly.

c **Equipment**

- Study Location and Documentation Data form (see Appendix A)
- Robel Pole form (see Illustration 5)
- Cover classes for the area or plant community
- Aerial photographs or management unit map
- Robel pole (see Illustration 6)

d **Training** The accuracy of the data depends on the training and ability of the examiners. They must receive adequate and consistent training in laying out transects, determining cover classes, and reading the Robel pole.

e **Establishing Studies** Careful establishment of studies is a critical element in obtaining meaningful data. Select key species and determine the number, length, and location of the transects (see Section III.B.7).

(1) Establish the number of visual cover classes and height limits for each class based on resource management objectives. These cover classes must be developed locally for each ecological site or plant community.

The following is an example of cover classes established for upland bird nesting cover on the Fort Pierre National Grasslands:

Cover Classes	Visual Obstruction Height
1	0.0 - 1.9
2	2.0 - 2.9
3	3.0 - 3.9
4	4.0 +

(2) Collect data using several pilot transects to determine the number of transects needed and the number of observations to be made on each transect. These data are needed to determine if a statistically valid sample has been collected (see Section III.B.7).

(3) At the beginning of each study, determine the transect bearing and distance between observation points. Select a prominent distant landmark such as a large tree, rocky point, etc., that can be used as the transect bearing point.

(4) Plot the transects on detailed management unit maps and/or aerial photos (see beginning of Section III).

(5) Permanently mark the location of each study with a reference post and study location stake (see beginning of Section III).

(6) Number studies for proper identification to ensure that the data collected can be positively associated with specific studies on the ground (see Appendix B).

(7) Document the location and other pertinent information concerning the study on the Study Location and Documentation Data form (see beginning of Section III and Appendix A).

f Sampling Process This technique can be most effectively accomplished utilizing two individuals.

(1) Start a transect by taking the specified number of paces along the transect bearing before making the first reading (observation point). Two Visual Observation (VO) measurements are taken at each observation point from opposite directions along the contour. One examiner holds the Robel pole at the observation point, while the second examiner holds the end of the cord perpendicular to the transect (see Illustration 6). The Visual Observation (VO) measurement is made by determining the highest 1-inch band totally or partially visible and then assigning the cover class. Record the cover class on the Robel Pole form (Illustration 5).

(2) Continue the transect by taking readings at the specified intervals along the transect bearing until the transect is complete. The distance between observation points can be increased to expand the area sampled.

g Calculations Total the Visual Observation measurements on the Robel Pole form (Illustration 5) for both readings at each observation points and record at the bottom of the form. Add these two totals and divide by the total number of readings.

h Data Analysis Calculate confidence intervals around average heights.

i References

Robel, R.J., J.N. Briggs, A.D.,Dayton, and L.C., Hulbert. 1970. Relationships Between Visual Obstruction Measurements and Weight of Grassland Vegetation, J. Range Manage. 23:295.

Robel, R.J. 1970. Possible Role of Behavior in Regulating Greater Prairie Chickens' Populations, J. Wildlife Manage. Vol 34 (2).

Snyder, W.D. 1991. Wheat stubble as nesting cover for ring necked pheasants in northern Colorado. Wildlife Soc. bulletin vol 19(4).

USDA, Forest Service. 1994. Rangeland Analysis and Management Training Guide, Rocky Mountain Region USDA Forest Service Denver, CO.

Robel Pole

Study Number			Date		Examiner		
Allotment Name & Number					Pasture		
Sampling Interval		Study Location					

Transect	#-		#-		#-		#-	
Station	VO	VO	VO	VO	VO	VO	VO	VO
1								
2								
3								
4								
5								
6								
7								
8								
9								
10								
11								
12								
13								
14								
15								
16								
17								
18								
19								
20								
21								
22								
23								
24								
25								
Total								
Grand Total								
Average								

Illustration 5   59

Robel Pole

Study Number	Sand Hill #1		Date	6/18/94		Examiner	Scott Taylor	

Allotment Name & Number Sand Hill 20216   Pasture 2

Sampling Interval 10 paces   Study Location 2 miles west of Walker Well on south side of the road.

Transect	#- 1		#-		#-		#-	
Station	VO	VO	VO	VO	VO	VO	VO	VO
1	1	3						
2	2	4						
3	1	1						
4	2	1						
5	3	1						
6	1	2						
7	3	4						
8	3	3						
9	4	4						
10	1	2						
11	2	3						
12	1	1						
13	2	1						
14	3	2						
15	2	3						
16	1	2						
17	2	2						
18	3	3						
19	2	4						
20	3	3						
21	3	2						
22	1	3						
23	2	2						
24	3	1						
25	2	2						
Total	53	59						
Grand Total	112							
Average	2.24							

Robel Pole

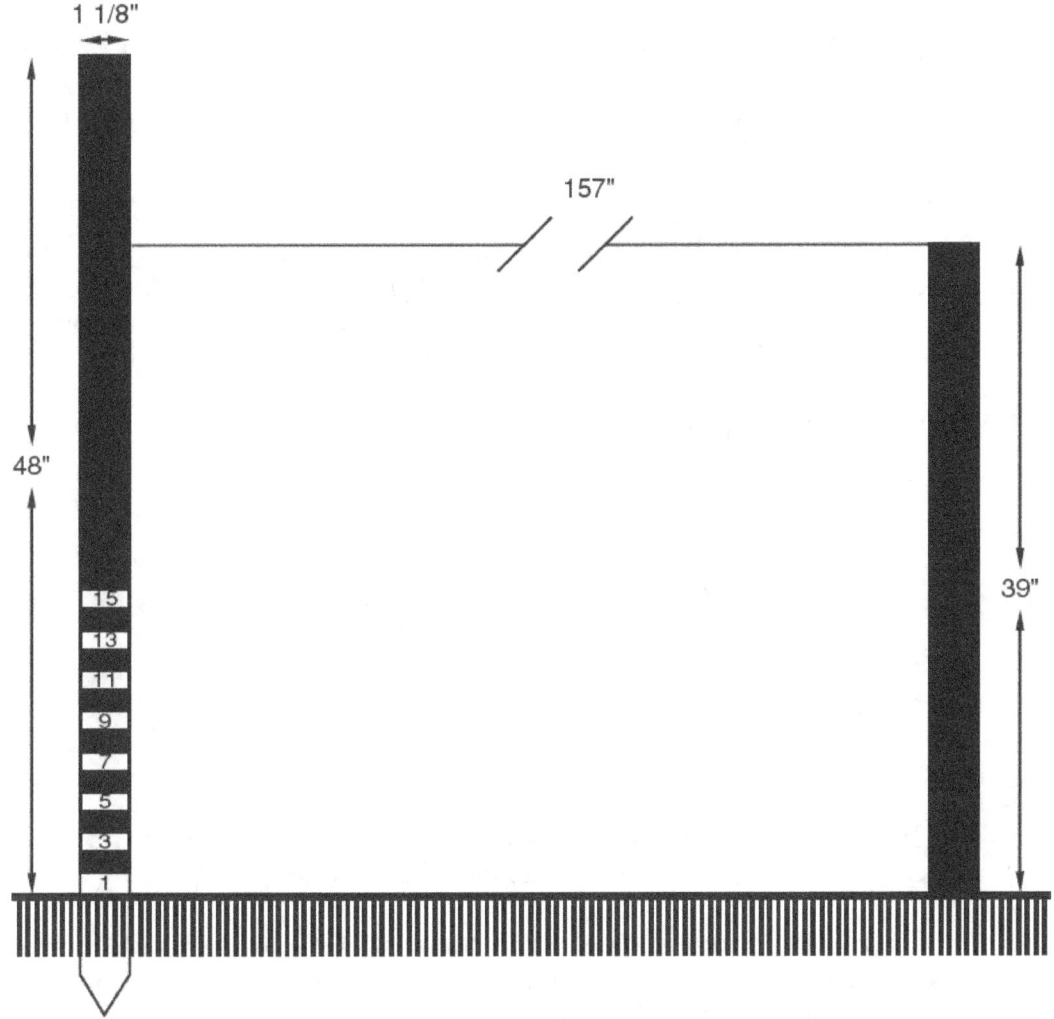

1 1/8"

157"

48"

39"

15
13
11
9
7
5
3
1

1. Pole is 1.125 inches in diameter and 48 inches long.

2. Pole is painted with alternating 1-inch bands of flat white and gray colors, starting with white on the bottom. Alternating 1-inch bands can be extended to the top of the pole if needed.

3. A single 157-inch (4m) cord is attached to the pole at a height of 39 inches (1m) to standardize the distance and height at which readings are taken.

4. Narrow black numbers corresponding to the number of bands are painted on the white bands. For example, the bottom white band is "1," the next white band is "3," and so on.

5. A spike is attached to the bottom of the pole so that it can be pushed into the ground, allowing one examiner to make the readings. The spike can be removed if not needed.

Illustration 6

61

3. *Comparative Yield Method* This method is used to estimate standing crop or production of a site remaining after a use period. The total production in a sample quadrat is compared to one of five reference quadrats; relative ranks are recorded rather than estimating the weight directly.

a **Areas of Use** This method works best for herbaceous vegetation but can also be used successfully with small shrubs and half-shrubs. As with most production estimates, the Comparative Yield method can be used to compare relative production between different sites.

b **Advantages and Limitations** The advantage of the comparative yield method is that a large number of samples can be obtained quickly. Total production is evaluated, so clipping calibration on a species basis is not needed. The process of developing reference quadrats for ranking purposes reduces both sampling and training time. Identification of individual species is not required.

Large-shrub vegetation communities are not well suited for this technique.

c **Equipment**

- Study Location and Documentation Data form (see Appendix A)
- Comparative Yield form (see Illustration 7)
- Five sampling quadrat frames (see Illustration 8)
- Clippers
- Paper bags
- Kilogram and gram spring-loaded scale with clip
- Compass

d **Training** Examiners must calibrate their estimates when sampling situations change (i.e., different sites, time of day, change of season).

e **Establishing Studies** Careful establishment of studies is a critical element in obtaining meaningful data. Select key species and determine the number, length, and location of the transects (see Section III.B.7). Depending on management objectives, comparative yield data can be collected on either permanent or temporary transects.

(1) Collect data using several pilot transects to determine the number of transects needed and the number of observations to be made on each transect. These data are needed to determine if a statistically valid sample has been collected (see Section III.B.7).

(2) The criteria for selecting the proper size quadrat are the same as for any weight estimate procedure (see the Interagency Technical Reference, *Sampling Vegetation Attributes*). Use the same size quadrat throughout a study.

(3) Establish one transect on each study site; establish more if needed. More than one transect may be required for each study site.

(4) At the study location, determine the transect bearing and select a prominent distant landmark such as a peak, rocky point, etc., that can be used as the transect bearing point.

(5) Number studies for proper identification to ensure that the data collected can be positively associated with specific studies on the ground (see Appendix B).

(6) Document the location and other pertinent information concerning the study on the Study Location and Documentation Data form (see beginning of Section III and Appendix A).

(7) Plot the transects on detailed management unit maps and/or aerial photos (see beginning of Section III).

(8) Permanently mark the location of each study with a reference post and study location stake (see beginning of Section III).

f Sampling Process

(1) A set of reference quadrats must be established. The sample quadrats will be compared and rated back to these reference quadrats. The reference quadrats represent the range in dry weight of standing crop that will be commonly found during sampling.

(a) Five reference quadrats are subjectively located. References 1 and 5 are located first. The first quadrat (reference 1) is placed in a low-yielding or the heaviest grazed area which represents the low-yielding situations commonly encountered on the site (avoid bare or nearly bare quadrats). Reference 5 is determined by placing a quadrat on a high-yielding area; exclude unusually dense patches of vegetation that would have a rare chance of being sampled. The examiner should make a mental note of the amount of production and level of utilization in each of the reference quadrats. These references are then clipped and weighed. If the clipped weight in reference 5 is more than five times the weight found in reference 1, then two new sites should be selected as references 1 and 5. In establishing the initial reference quadrats, the weight in reference 5 is usually too high and the weight in reference 1 is too low. Make sure reference 5 does not represent a rare situation. When references 1 and 5 have been selected, reference 3 is located by placing a frame in an area considered to have a yield halfway between references 1 and 5. References 2 and 4 are located the same way by selecting the mid-point yield between references 1 and 3 and references 3 and 5, respectively.

(b) All five quadrats are clipped and weighed to compare the reference quadrats to a linear distribution of quadrat weights. This process is repeated by clipping additional quadrats until the weights of the five reference quadrats are approximately linear and observers are confident in their ability to rank quadrats relative to one of the five references. If the rankings are not linear, the precision of the method will be reduced. If more than five percent of the quadrats have no production, then a larger quadrat frame should be used.

(c) In areas with less than 500 lb/ac, small quadrats are difficult to evaluate. In these situations, either larger quadrats should be used or three reference quadrats should be established instead of five.

(2) *Collecting the Data*

(a) Start a transect by randomly selecting a point in the study site, taking five paces along the transect bearing, and then ranking the first quadrat.

(b) Read additional quadrats at specified intervals. To change the length of the transect, increase the number of paces between quadrats.

(c) For each quadrat, compare the total yield in the quadrat to the references and record the appropriate rank by dot count tally. It is appropriate to assign intermediate ranks if the yield is at the midpoint between two references. For example, if a quadrat has a yield between references 1 and 2, assign a rank of 1.5. If a quadrat yield greatly exceeds the yield of reference 5, then a higher rank may be estimated. For example, if a quadrat is 50% greater than reference 5, a rank of 7 could be recorded. If more than five percent of the quadrats are ranked above 5, the references were not properly selected.

(d) To calibrate the ranks, several quadrats representing each reference should be clipped and weighed independently of the transect line. The total yield in each quadrat is determined without regard to species. Be sure to save all clipped material. The reference quadrats can be used as part of these clipped quadrats. The more quadrats clipped, the better the calibration. Each distinct sampling period should have a separate calibration. Bags can be weighed in the field to determine green weight and then saved and dried to determine dry weight. These weights are then used to determine average weight per reference.

(e) It is recommended that 100 to 200 quadrats be ranked for each site.

g Calculations The number of quadrats tallied for each ranking is totaled (Illustration 7, column 2) and multiplied by the ranking (column 1).

Rank x Tally = Weighted ranking

These weighted rankings (column 3) are summed and divided by the number of total quadrats. This indicates the average ranking for the site.

$$\frac{\text{Total rank}}{\text{Total number of quadrats sampled}} = \text{Average ranking for the site}$$

The average yield may be estimated with a ratio estimate (described below) or a least-squares regression technique. The ratio estimate is good for quick field calculations, but the least-squares regression should be used for final data analysis.

To use the ratio estimate technique, calculate the average rank and average clipped weight of the harvested quadrats by dividing the total of the clipped rankings and the total clipped weight by the number of harvested (clipped) quadrats (column 4 and 5).

$$\frac{\text{Total of clipped rankings}}{\text{Total number of clipped quadrats}} = \text{Average rank of clipped quadrats}$$

$$\frac{\text{Total clipped weight}}{\text{Total number of clipped quadrats}} = \text{Average weight of clipped quadrats}$$

The average clipped weight is then divided by the average rank to determine the average rank interval.

$$\frac{\text{Average weight of clipped quadrats}}{\text{Average rank of clipped quadrats}} = \text{Average rank interval (ARI)}$$

The average ranking for the site—which is based on the *estimated*, not clipped, quadrats—is then multiplied by the average rank interval to estimate the average yield per quadrat for the site.

Average ranking for the site **x** Average rank interval = Average yield/Quadrat.

The average yield in grams per quadrat obtained above can be converted to either pounds/acre or kilograms/hectare.

Use the following table to convert grams to pounds per acre if the total area sampled is a multiple of 9.6 ft^2.

Table 1

(# of quadrats x size = total area)		
(10 x 0.96 = 9.6 ft^2)	multiply grams times 10.0 =	pounds per acre
(10 x 1.92 = 19.2 ft^2)	multiply grams times 5.0 =	pounds per acre
(10 x 2.4 = 24.0 ft^2)	multiply grams times 4.0 =	pounds per acre
(10 x 4.8 = 48.0 ft^2)	multiply grams times 2.0 =	pounds per acre
(10 x 9.6 = 96.0 ft^2)	multiply grams times 1.0 =	pounds per acre
(10 x 96.0 = 960.0 ft^2)	multiply grams times 0.1 =	pounds per acre

To convert to kilograms per hectare, first determine the number of quadrats in a hectare by dividing the number of square meters in a hectare (10,000 m^2) by the total area (in square meters) of the quadrat. Then divide the number of quadrats in a hectare by 1,000 to arrive at the conversion factor used to convert grams per quadrat into kilograms per hectare.

For example, if the quadrat size is 40 x 40 centimeters (0.4 x 0.4 meters), then the quadrat area would be 0.4 multiplied by 0.4, or .16 m^2. The number of quadrats in a hectare is calculated by dividing 10,000 by .16, which works out to 62,500 quadrats per acre. Dividing this number by 1,000 results in the conversion factor, which is 62.5. The final step is to multiply the average yield per quadrat obtained from the final equation above by 62.5 to arrive at kilograms per hectare.

h Data Analysis Calculate confidence intervals around the estimate of average pounds per acre or kilograms per hectare.

i References

Despain, D.W., P.R. Ogden, and E.L. Smith. 1991. Plant frequency sampling for monitoring rangelands. In: G.B. Ruyle, ed. Some Methods for Monitoring Rangelands and other Natural Area Vegetation. Extension Report 9043, University of Arizona, College of Agriculture, Tucson, AZ.

Comparative Yield

Study Number		Date	Examiner		Pasture

Allotment Name & Number		Number of Quadrats		Quadrat Size

Study Location

Sampled Quadrats			Harvested Quadrat	
Rank (1)	Tally (2)	Rank x Tally (3)	Clip Rank (4)	Clip Weight (5)
0				
.5				
1				
1.5				
2				
2.5				
3				
3.5				
4				
4.5				
5				
Total				
Average				

Notes

Illustration 7   67

Comparative Yield

Study Number	Silver Creek #4	Date 8/9/95	Examiner Wally Pip	Pasture 3

Allotment Name & Number	Silver Creek 21703	Number of Quadrats 25	Quadrat Size 40 x 40

Study Location 2 miles east of Red Well on north side of road

Sampled Quadrats			Harvested Quadrat	
Rank (1)	Tally (2)	Rank x Tally (3)	Clip Rank (4)	Clip Weight (5)
0	0	0	1	10
.5	0	0	2	27
1	3	3	3	46
1.5	4	6	4	62
2	5	10	5	83
2.5	4	10		
3	2	6		
3.5	3	10.5		
4	2	8		
4.5	1	4.5		
5	1	5		
Total	25	63	15	228
Average		2.52	3	45.6

Notes

Illustration 7

Comparative Yield Quadrat Frame

The frame is made of 3/8-inch
iron rod and 1-inch angle iron
or 1 1/4-inch x 3/16-inch flat iron.

Quadrat size should be based on local conditions
determined from the pilot study.

QUADRAT

Number	Size		Area
1	7.5 x 7.5	cm	56.25 sq cm
2	15.0 x 15.0	cm	225.00 sq cm
3	30.0 x 30.0	cm	900.00 sq cm
4	40.0 x 40.0	cm	1600.00 sq cm
5	50.0 x 50.0	cm	2500.00 sq cm
6	20.0 x 50.0	cm	1000.00 sq cm

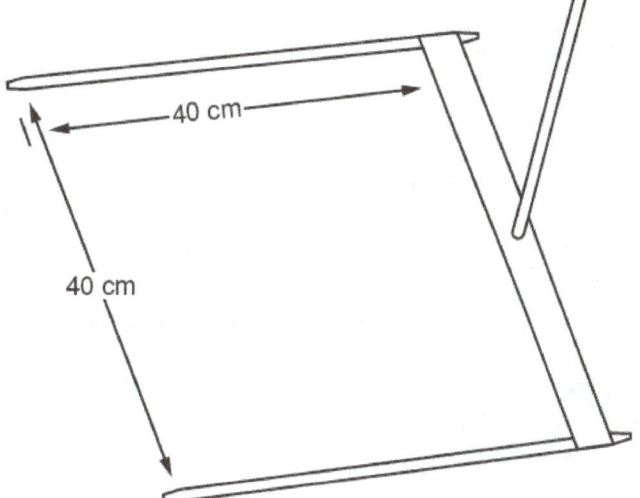

40 cm

40 cm

Illustration 8

69

C. Herbaceous Removal Methods

1. Paired Plot Method Under the Paired Plot Method, forage from protected and unprotected plots is clipped and weighed at the end of the use period. The difference between these two weights represents the amount of forage consumed or otherwise destroyed during that period.

a Areas of Use This method is suitable for all vegetation growth forms for which production and utilization data are commonly desired. It is particularly applicable where periods of use are short, use is relatively uniform, and regrowth after foraging is not significant.

b Advantages and Disadvantages

(1) This method is a simple and direct way of measuring utilization.

(2) Little training is required and accuracy is generally high.

(3) This method is time consuming, and ungrazed areas that are protected from foraging are required.

(4) Where periods of use are long, this method does not provide information about the cumulative production of foraged plants unless the cages are moved at short time intervals.

(5) New plots must always be established once the study plots have been clipped.

c Equipment

- Study Location and Documentation Data form (see Appendix A)
- Paired Plot form (see Illustration 9)
- Frames to delineate plots
- Portable cages to protect plots (see Appendix E)
- Stakes for anchoring cages
- Hammer
- Clipping shears
- Paper sacks
- Spring scale, calibrated in grams

d Training The Paired Plot Method does not require intensive field training, although examiners must be able to identify plant species. Examiners can perform the clipping and weighing procedures after only a short training period.

e Establishing Studies Careful establishment of studies is a critical element in obtaining meaningful data. Select key species and determine the number, length, and location of the transects (see Section III.B.7).

(1) Collect data using several pilot transects to determine the number of transects needed and the number of observations to be made on each

transect. These data are needed to determine if a statistically valid sample has been collected (see Section III.B.7).

(2) *Site selection and layout.*

    (a) Select plots to be examined at random (see Section III.B.2).

    (b) The number of plots selected depends on the purpose for which the estimates are to be used, uniformity of the vegetation, and other factors. (See Section III.B.7 for statistical considerations.)

    (c) Adapt the size and shape of plots to the vegetation community to be sampled.

(3) Anchor a cage over one of the paired plots at each plot location. See Appendix E for examples of several kinds of utilization cages. The base of a cage should be large enough to provide at least a 6-inch buffer zone between the edge of the plot and the side of the cage. The lower portion of the cage (to approximately 1 to 2 feet high) may be covered with net wire small enough to exclude rabbits and rodents. Generally, the larger the mesh, the less influence the cage has in modifying the environment.

(4) Protected plots may be located in exclosures. These plots need not be caged unless it is necessary to exclude rabbits and rodents.

    (a) If protected plots are located within permanent exclosures, caution must be exercised to ensure that these plots are representative of the unforaged situation outside the exclosures. Plant composition and growth must be similar. The area inside a permanent exclosure may have a different environment due to nonuse.

    (b) Protected plots may be located within temporary exclosures, such as exclosures constructed with electric fence. Plots protected by temporary exclosures can be moved every year to eliminate the artificial environment created by continued non-use in permanent exclosures.

(5) Leave one plot of each pair open to foraging. If past experience shows that foraging is particularly uneven, leave two or more plots open for each one caged in order to average the unevenly foraged conditions. Animals are attracted to cages and may trample unprotected plots if located too near protected plots. Therefore, establish unprotected plots a minimum of 100 feet from protected plots. Unprotected plots should be inconspicuously marked to avoid attracting animals.

(6) Plot the transects on detailed management unit maps and/or aerial photos (see beginning of Section III).

(7) Permanently mark the location of each study with a reference post and study location stake (see beginning of Section III).

(8) Number studies for proper identification to ensure that the data collected can be positively associated with specific studies on the ground (see Appendix B).

(9) Document the location and other pertinent information concerning the study on the Study Location and Documentation Data form (see beginning of Section III and Appendix A).

f Sampling Process After examiners are trained, proceed with the collection of utilization data.

(1) Clip the current year's growth on key species from protected and unprotected plots.

(2) On herbaceous species, clip all current year's growth to within 1 inch of the ground to save the root crown.

(3) On browse species, remove all current year's growth available for foraging animals. For large browse plants, the available current year's growth may be removed from part of the plant rather then from the whole plant. The portion of the browse removed is then converted to total weight based on sample size. (Example: If one-fourth of the available current year's growth of browse plants is removed, the weight of the browse removed times four equals the total weight.)

(4) Put the clippings from the protected and unprotected plots in separate paper sacks for weighing.

(5) Weigh the sacks of clipped plants and record separately the weight from the protected and unprotected plots on the Paired Plot form (see Illustration 9). Subtract the weight of the sack before recording the weights of the plants.

g Calculations

(1) Calculate the percent utilization as follows:

$$\% \text{ utilization} = \frac{\text{Total protected weight} - \text{Total unprotected weight}}{\text{Total protected weight}} \times 100$$

(2) If an unequal number of protected and unprotected plots are used in the study, calculate the percent utilization as follows:

$$\% \text{ utilization} = \frac{\text{Average weight for protected plots} - \text{Average weight for unprotected plots}}{\text{Average weight for protected plots}} \times 100$$

(3) Record the percent utilization on the Paired Plot form (see Illustration 9).

h Data Analysis Calculate confidence intervals around the estimate of average percent utilization.

i References

Frischknecht, Neil C. and Paul W. Conrad. 1965. Adaptable, transportable utilization cages. J. Range Manage. 18:33-34.

U.S. Department of Interior Bureau of Land Management. 1984. Rangeland Monitoring - Utilization Studies, TR4400-3.

Paired Plot

Study Number		Date	Examiner

Allotment Name & Number	Pasture

Kind and/or Class of Animal	Period of Use

Key Species	Plot	Weight in grams by plot					Total Average Utilization (sum of percent utilization per pair divided by total number pairs)
		1	2	3	4	5	
1	P*						
	U**						
	P - U						
	$\frac{P-U}{P} \times 100$						
2	P*						
	U**						
	P - U						
	$\frac{P-U}{P} \times 100$						
3	P*						
	U**						
	P - U						
	$\frac{P-U}{P} \times 100$						
4	P*						
	U**						
	P - U						
	$\frac{P-U}{P} \times 100$						

Location of Paired Plot 1	Location of Paired Plot 2

Location of Paired Plot 3	Location of Paired Plot 4

Location of Paired Plot 5

* Protected Plots   ** Unprotected Plots

Notes (Use other side or another page if necessary)

Illustration 9

Paired Plot

Study Number	Date	Examiner
21S – 1W – 27 – 03	9/5/95	Hank Aaron

Allotment Name & Number	Pasture
Box Canyon 13105	Home

Kind and/or Class of Animal	Period of Use
Cattle	5/1 to 8/30

Key Species	Plot	Weight in grams by plot					Total Average Utilization (sum of percent utilization per pair divided by total number pairs)
		1	2	3	4	5	
1 BOER 2	P*	25	40	38	30	28	47 %
	U**	15	25	15	18	12	
	P - U	10	15	23	12	16	
	$\frac{P-U}{P}$ x 100	.40	.37	.60	.40	.57	
2 BOCU	P*	30	28	19	43	25	55 %
	U**	16	13	8	17	11	
	P - U	14	15	11	26	14	
	$\frac{P-U}{P}$ x 100	.47	.54	.58	.60	.56	
3	P*						
	U**						
	P - U						
	$\frac{P-U}{P}$ x 100						
4	P*						
	U**						
	P - U						
	$\frac{P-U}{P}$ x 100						

Location of Paired Plot 1 Caged plot is 1.5 miles south of Coyote well – then 300 ft. west of road. Uncaged plot is 700 feet SW of caged plot.

Location of Paired Plot 2 Caged plot is 1500 feet north of caged plot 1. Uncaged plot is 150 feet west of caged plot.

Location of Paired Plot 3 Caged plot is 1.7 miles west of Spring Creek Reservoir. Uncaged plot is 75 paces north of caged plots.

Location of Paired Plot 4 Caged plot is 500 paces south of caged plot 3. Uncaged plot is 50 paces east of the caged plot.

Location of Paired Plot 5 Caged plot is .3 miles north of Buck brush cattleguard – then 700 feet east of road. Uncaged plot is 200 feet north of caged plot.

* Protected Plots	** Unprotected Plots

Notes (Use other side or another page if necessary)

Illustration 9   75

2. *Ocular Estimate* With the Ocular Estimate Method, utilization is determined along a transect by ocular estimate. The percentage by weight of forage removed is determined for individual plants of the key species or from all plants of the key species within small quadrats.

a **Areas of Use** This method has wide applicability and is suited for use with both grasses and forbs.

b **Advantages and Limitations**

(1) The most important advantage is speed.

(2) The method is reasonably accurate, depending upon the ability of the examiners.

(3) Vegetation is not disturbed.

(4) Reliability of estimates is increased by limiting observations to individual plants or small areas (quadrats).

(5) Errors in personal judgement on individual plants or quadrats frequently tend to be compensating.

(6) A limitation is that exclosures, cages, or fenced areas may be needed for training.

c **Equipment**

- Study Location and Documentation Data form (see Appendix A)
- Ocular Estimate form (see Illustration 10)
- Frames to delineate quadrats (if necessary)
- Clipping shears
- Paper sacks
- Spring scale, calibrated in grams
- Cages as required (see Appendix E)

d **Training** The accuracy of estimating utilization percentages is depends upon thoroughness of training and the ability of examiners to identify plant species and the amount of use. The examiners must first compare ocular estimates against actual weight values obtained by clipping and weighing (see Section III.D.9).

(1) *Locating training sites* Locate sites for training purposes on similar unforaged or protected sites. If it is unlikely that a site containing unforaged vegetation will be available after the foraging season, it will be necessary to construct temporary exclosures or install cages on study sites prior to the period of use.

(2) *Making ocular estimates* Training involves estimating utilization on individual plants of the key species or on all plants of the key species within a small quadrat. If quadrats are to be used for the studies, use quadrats of the same size for training. The quadrats should be small

enough so that the entire quadrat is clearly visible to the examiner. Examiners should practice making ocular estimates as follows:

(a) Clip individual plants of the key species, or plants of key species on a quadrat, to simulate foraging (sample A).

(b) Estimate the percentage of weight removed.

(c) Clip the remaining forage of the selected plants by removing all current year's growth available to the foraging animals (sample B).

(d) Put the clippings for samples A and B in separate sacks

(e) Weigh samples A and B separately and subtract sack weight from the weight of each sample.

(f) Calculate the percent simulated use by dividing the weight of sample A by the combined weight of samples A and B and multiplying the value by 100.

(g) Compare estimates with actual percent forage removed and determine the error of the estimates. Continue training until examiners can recognize the different percentages of use.

(3) ***Checking ocular estimates*** Training checks should be made and recorded each day prior to field estimation. This gives a permanent record of the accuracy of each examiner's ocular estimates.

e **Establishing Studies** Careful establishment of studies is a critical element in obtaining meaningful data. Select key species and determine the number, length, and location of the transects (see Section III.B.7).

(1) Collect data using several pilot transects to determine the number of transects needed and the number of observations to be made on each transect. These data are needed to determine if a statistically valid sample has been collected (see Section III.B.7).

(2) At the beginning of each study, determine the transect bearing and distance between observation points. Select a prominent distant landmark such as a large tree, rocky point, etc., that can be used as the transect bearing point.

(3) Plot the transects on detailed management unit maps and/or aerial photos (see beginning of Section III).

(4) Permanently mark the location of each study with a reference post and study location stake (see beginning of Section III).

(5) Number studies for proper identification to ensure that the data collected can be positively associated with specific studies on the ground (see Appendix B).

(6) Document the location and other pertinent information concerning the study on the Study Location and Documentation Data form (see beginning of Section III and Appendix A).

f **Sampling Process** After examiners are trained and are confident in their ability to recognize degrees of utilization, proceed with the collection of utilization data.

(1) At each interval along a transect, select the plant of the key species nearest the toe and estimate and record the percent utilization.

(2) If a quadrat is used, place the frame immediately in front of the toe and then estimate and record the percent utilization. If the key species does not occur in the quadrat, proceed along the transect until the key species is encountered. A quadrat is particularly important for mat- or sod-forming grasses or forbs.

(3) Record the percent utilization on the Ocular Estimate form (see Illustration 10).

g **Calculations** Calculate the average percent utilization by totaling the utilization estimates for the plants or quadrats along the transect and dividing the total by the number of sampled plants or quadrats. Record the average utilization on the Ocular Estimate form (see Illustration 10).

h **Data Analysis** Calculate confidence intervals around the estimate of average percent utilization.

i **References**

Reid, E.H. and G.D. Pickford. 1941. A comparison of the ocular-estimate by-plot and the stubble-height methods for determining percentage utilization of range grasses. J. Forestry 39:935-941.

U.S. Department of Interior Bureau of Land Management. 1984. Rangeland Monitoring - Utilization Studies, TR4400-3.

Ocular Estimate

Study Number		Date	Examiner

Allotment Name & Number	Pasture

Kind and/or Class of Animal	Period of Use

Key Species	Ocular estimates by plant (or plot)															Total
	1	2	3	4	5	6	7	8	9	10	11	12	13	14	15	

Total ÷ no. of samples (plants or plots) = avg. percent utilization   ÷   =

Notes (Use other side or another page, if necessary)

Key Species	Ocular estimates by plant (or plot)															Total
	1	2	3	4	5	6	7	8	9	10	11	12	13	14	15	

Total ÷ no. of samples (plants or plots) = avg. percent utilization   ÷   =

Notes (Use other side or another page, if necessary)

Illustration 10   79

Ocular Estimate

Study Number	Date	Examiner
O3S - 27W - 08 - 04	7/18/95	Joe Jackson

Allotment Name & Number	Pasture
Quaking Aspen - 30134	Sheep Creek

Kind and/or Class of Animal	Period of Use
Cattle	5/16 to 7/15

Key Species	Ocular estimates by plant (or plot)															
	1	2	3	4	5	6	7	8	9	10	11	12	13	14	15	Total
AGSP	60	35	40	50	70	25	30	40	65	80	50	75	70	40	30	760
	55	40	60	70	65	50	40	60	75	40	30	55	55	60	70	825
	85	75	80	65	50	45	50	70	65	60	40	50	60	65	45	905
	65	50	70	40	35											

Total ÷ no. of samples (plants or plots) = avg. percent utilization   2750 ÷ 50   = 55 %

Notes (Use other side or another page, if necessary)

There is no evidence of recent or active erosion. Numerous AGSP seedings are present. The permittee, Ed Barnes, helped collect the data.

Key Species	Ocular estimates by plant (or plot)															
	1	2	3	4	5	6	7	8	9	10	11	12	13	14	15	Total

Total ÷ no. of samples (plants or plots) = avg. percent utilization   ÷   =

Notes (Use other side or another page, if necessary)

3. *Key Species Method (formerly the Modified Key Forage Plant Method)* This technique is a combination of the Landscape Appearance Method (Section V.D) and the Ocular Estimate Method (Section V.C.2). Utilization levels are based on an ocular estimate of the amount of forage removed by weight on individual key species and observations are recorded in one of seven utilization classes.

a **Areas of Use** This method is adapted to areas where perennial grasses, forbs, and/or browse plants are the key species.

b **Advantages and Limitations** This method is rapid. The estimated percentage of forage removed is recorded in one of seven broad classes rather than as a precise amount. The method is also reasonably accurate, depending upon the ability of the examiners. Different examiners are more likely to estimate utilization in the same classes than to estimate the same utilization percentages. Vegetation is not disturbed. Reliability of estimates is increased by limiting observations to individual plants or small areas (quadrats). A limitation is that exclosures, cages, or fenced areas may be needed for training.

c **Equipment**

- Study Location and Documentation Data form (see Appendix A)
- Key Species form (see Illustration 11)
- Tally counter (optional)
- Frames to delineate quadrats (if necessary)
- Clipping shears
- Paper sacks
- Spring scale, calibrated in grams
- Cages as required (see Appendix E)

d **Training** The accuracy of estimating utilization percentages depends upon thoroughness of training and the ability of examiners to identify plant species and the amount of use. The examiners must first compare their ocular estimates against actual weight values obtained by clipping and weighing (see Section III.D.9).

(1) *Locating training sites* Locate sites for training purposes on similar unforaged or protected sites. If it is unlikely that a site containing unforaged vegetation will be available after the foraging season, it will be necessary to construct temporary exclosures or install cages on study sites prior to the period of use.

(2) *Making ocular estimates* Training involves estimating utilization on individual plants of the key species or on all plants of the key species on a small quadrat. If quadrats are to be used for the studies, use quadrats of the same size for training. The quadrats should be small enough so that the entire quadrat is clearly visible to the examiner. Examiners should practice making ocular estimates as follows:

(a) Clip individual plants of the key species, or plants of the key species on a quadrat, to simulate foraging (sample A).

(b) Estimate the percentage of weight removed.

(c) Clip the remaining forage of the selected plants by removing all current year's growth available to the foraging animals (sample B).

(d) Put the clippings for samples A and B in separate paper sacks.

(e) Weigh samples A and B separately and subtract sack weight from the weight of each sample.

(f) Calculate the percent simulated use by dividing the weight of sample A by the combined weight of samples A and B and multiplying the value by 100.

(g) Compare estimates with the actual percent forage removed and determine the error of the estimates. Continue training until examiners can recognize the different percentages of use.

(3) *Identifying utilization classes* Examiners must be able to recognize the seven herbaceous or seven browse utilization classes using the written class descriptions.

e **Establishing Studies** Careful establishment of studies is a critical element in obtaining meaningful data. Select key species and determine the number, length, and location of the transects (see Section III.B.7).

(1) Collect data using several pilot transects to determine the number of transects needed and the number of observations to be made on each transect. These data are needed to determine if a statistically valid sample has been collected (see Section III.B.7).

(2) At the beginning of each study, determine the transect bearing and distance between observation points. Select a prominent distant landmark such as a large tree, rocky point, etc., that can be used as the transect bearing point.

(3) Plot the transects on detailed management unit maps and/or aerial photos (see beginning of Section III).

(4) Permanently mark the location of each study with a reference post and study location stake (see beginning of Section III).

(5) Number studies for proper identification to ensure that the data collected can be positively associated with specific studies on the ground (see Appendix B).

(6) Document the location and other pertinent information concerning the study on the Study Location and Documentation Data form (see beginning of Section III and Appendix A).

f **Sampling Process** After examiners are trained and are confident in their ability to recognize various degrees of utilization, proceed with the collection of utilization data.

(1) *Sampling techniques*

(a) At each interval along a transect, select the plant of the key species nearest the toe and estimate and record the percent utilization by weight.

(b) If a quadrat is being used, place the frame immediately in front of the toe and estimate and record the percent utilization. If the key species does not occur in the quadrat, proceed along the transect until the key species is encountered.

(c) Record each observation by dot count in the appropriate utilization class on the Key Species form (see Illustration 11).

(2) *Herbaceous utilization classes* Seven utilization classes are used to show relative degrees of use of key herbaceous species (grasses and forbs). Each class represents a numerical range of percent utilization. Utilization estimates must be placed in one of the seven classes. Utilization classes are as follows:

(a) (0-5%). The key species show no evidence of grazing use or negligible use.

(b) (6-20%). The key species has the appearance of very light grazing. Plants may be topped or slightly used. Current seedstalks and young plants are little disturbed.

(c) (21-40%). The key species may be topped, skimmed, or grazed in patches. Between 60 and 80 percent of current seedstalks remain intact. Most young plants are undamaged.

(d) (41-60%). Half of the available forage (by weight)on key species appears to have been utilized. Fifteen to 25 percent of current seedstalks remain intact.

(e) (61-80%). More than half of the available forage on key species appears to have been utilized. Less than 10 percent of the current seedstalks remain. Shoots of rhizomatous grasses are missing.

(f) (81-94). The key species appears to have been heavily utilized and there are indications of repeated use. There is no evidence of reproduction or current seedstalks.

(g) (95-100). The key species appears to have been completely utilized. The remaining stubble is utilized to the soil surface.

(3) *Browse Utilization Classes* Seven utilization classes show relative degrees of use of available current year's growth (leaders) of key browse plants (shrubs, half shrubs, woody vines, and trees). Each class represents a numerical range of percent utilization. Estimate utilization within one of the seven classes. Utilization classes are as follows:

(a) (0-5%). The key browse plants show no evidence of grazing use or only negligible use.

(b) (6-20%). The key browse plants have the appearance of very light use. The available leaders are little disturbed.

(c) (21-40%). There is obvious evidence of leader use. The available leaders appear cropped or browsed in patches and 60 to 80% of the available leader growth remains intact.

(d) (41-60%). Key browse plants appear rather uniformly utilized and 40 to 60% of the available leader growth remains intact.

(e) (61-80%). The key browse plants are hedged and some plant clumps may be slightly broken. Nearly all available leaders are used and few terminal buds remain. Between 20 and 40% of the available leader growth remains intact.

(f) (81-94%). There are indications the key browse species have been utilized repeatedly. There is no evidence of terminal buds and usually less than 20% of available leader growth remains intact. Some, and often much, of the second and third years' growth has been utilized. Hedging is readily apparent. Key browse plants frequently have broken branches.

(g) (95-100). Less than 5% of the available leader growth on the key browse plants remain intact. Most of the second and third years' growth have been utilized. All key browse plants have major portions broken.

g Calculations Calculate the percent utilization as follows:

(1) Convert the dot count to the number of observations for each utilization class.

(2) Multiply the number of observations in each utilization class times the midpoints of the class intervals.

(3) Total the products for all classes.

(4) Divide the sum by the total number of observations on the transect.

(5) Record the average percent utilization on the Key Species form (see Illustration 11).

h Data Analysis Calculate confidence intervals around the estimate of average percent utilization.

i References

Anderson, E. William and Wilbur F. Currier. 1973. Evaluating zones of utilization. J. Range Manage. 26:87-91.

Heady, Harold F. 1949. Methods of determining utilization of range forage. J. Range Manage. 2:53-63.

U.S. Department of Interior Bureau of Land Management. 1984. Rangeland Monitoring - Utilization Studies, TR4400-3.

Key Species

Study Number		Date	Examiner

Allotment Name & Number	Pasture

Kind and/or Class of Animal	Period of Use

Class Interval	Int Mid (M)	Key Species			Key Species		
		Dot Count	No. By Class (C)	No. X Midmt. (C)(M)	Dot Count	No. By Class (C)	No. X Midpt. (C)(M)
0-5%	2.5						
6-20%	13						
21-40%	30						
41-60%	50						
61-80%	70						
81-94%	88						
95-100%	97.5						
		Totals			Totals		
Avg. Util. $= \dfrac{\Sigma(CM)^*}{\Sigma C}$		_____ =			_____ =		

(a) (0-5%). The key species show no evidence of grazing use or negligible use.

(b) (6-20%). The key species has the appearance of very light grazing. Plants may be topped or slightly used. Current seedstalks and young plants are little disturbed.

(c) (21-40%). The key species may be topped, skimmed, or grazed in patches. Between 60 and 80 percent of current seedstalks remain intact. Most young plants are undamaged.

(d) (41-60%). Half of the available forage (by weight) on key species appears to have been utilized. Fifteen to 25 percent of current seedstalks remain intact.

(e) (61-80%). More than half of the available forage on key species appears to have been utilized. Less than 10 percent of the current seedstalks remain. Shoots of rhizomatous grasses are missing.

(f) (81-94%). The key species appear to have been heavily utilized and there are indications of repeated use. There is no evidence of reproduction or current seedstalks.

(g) (95-100%). The key species appears to have been completely utilized. The remaining stubble is utilized to the soil surface.

Notes (use other side or another page, if necessary)

* Where C = The number of observations within each class interval (C column),
M = the class interval midpoint (M column), and Σ = the summation symbol.

Illustration 11

Browse Utilization Classes

1. (0-5%). The key browse plants show no evidence of grazing use or only negligible use.

2. (6-20%). The key browse plants have the appearance of very light use. The available leaders are little disturbed.

3. (21-40%). There is obvious evidence of leader use. The available leaders appear cropped or browsed in patches and 60 to 80% of the available leader growth remains intact.

4. (41-60%). Key browse plants appear rather uniformly utilized and 40 to 60% of the available leader growth remains intact.

5. (61-80%). The key browse plants are hedged and some plant clumps may be slightly broken. Nearly all available leaders are used and few terminal buds remain. Between 20 and 40% of the available leader growth remains intact.

6. (81-94%). There are indications the key browse species have been utilized repeatedly. There is no evidence of terminal buds and usually less than 20% of available leader growth remains intact. Some, and often much, of the second and third years' growth has been utilized. Hedging is readily apparent. Key browse plants frequently have broken branches.

7. (95-100). Less than 5% of the available leader growth on the key browse plants remains intact. Most of the second and third years' growth has been utilized. All key browse plants have major portions broken.

Illustration 11 *page 2*   87

Key Species

Study Number	Date	Examiner
Moon Creek #1	*8/1/95*	*Brian Taylor*

Allotment Name & Number	Pasture
Moon Creek – 10817	

Kind and/or Class of Animal	Period of Use
Cattle	*5/1 to 7/30*

Class Interval	Int Mid (M)	Key Species *BOCU*			Key Species			
		Dot Count	No. By Class (C)	No. X Midmt. (C)(M)	Dot Count	No. By Class (C)	No. X Midpt. (C)(M)	
0-5%	2.5	⌐	6	15				(a) (0-5%). The key species show no evidence of grazing use or negligible use.
6-20%	13	∴	4	52				(b) (6-20%). The key species has the appearance of very light grazing. Plants may be topped or slightly used. Current seedstalks and young plants are little disturbed.
21-40%	30	⊠⌐.	16	480				(c) (21-40%). The key species may be topped, skimmed, or grazed in patches. Between 60 and 80 percent of current seedstalks remain intact. Most young plants are undamaged.
41-60%	50	⊠··	12	600				(d) (41-60%). Half of the available forage (by weight) on key species appears to have been utilized. Fiftee to 25 percent of current seedstalks remain intact.
61-80%	70	··	2	140				(e) (61-80%). More than half of the available forage on key species appears to have been utilized. Less than 10 percent of the current seedstalks remain. Shoots of rhizomatous grasses are missing.
81-94%	88							(f) (81-94%). The key species appear to have been heavily utilized and there are indications of repeated use. There is no evidence of reproduction or current seedstalks.
95-100%	97.5							(g) (95-100%). The key species appears to have been completely utilized. The remaining stubble is utilized to the soil surface.
		Totals	40	1287	Totals			

Avg. Util. = $\dfrac{\Sigma(CM)*}{\Sigma C}$ $\dfrac{1287}{40} = 32\%$ _____ =

Notes (use other side or another page, if necessary)

The ranch foreman, Bud Gloss, participated in the collection of data. He felt the average % utilization reflected the amount of use.

* Where C = The number of observations within each class interval (C column),
M = the class interval midpoint (M column), and Σ = the summation symbol.

4. *Height-Weight Method* The Height-Weight Method involves the measurement of heights of ungrazed and grazed grass or grasslike plants to determine average utilization. Measurements of plant heights recorded along transects are converted to percent of weight utilized by means of a utilization gauge (Lommasson and Jensen 1943). The utilization gauge is developed from height-weight relationship curves. This method provides a mechanical tool which can be used for training, checking personal judgment, and promoting uniformity of results between examiners, as well as for determining percent utilization.

a **Areas of Use** This method is adapted for obtaining utilization data where the key species are either bunch or rhizomatous/sod-forming grasses or grasslike species.

b **Advantages and Limitations** This method provides uniform, accurate, and reliable utilization determinations for perennial grasses and grasslike species. It is an objective method; however, some estimation is required. This method requires numerous ungrazed plants, which may be hard to locate. Accurate utilization scales may not be available for the key species. The development of the height-weight relationship curves and preparation of utilization gauges scales can be time-consuming. This method cannot be used for determining utilization of forbs and shrubs.

c **Equipment**

- Study Location and Documentation Data form (see Appendix A)
- Height-Weight form (see Illustration 12)
- Utilization gauge (see Illustration 13)
- Utilization scales for key species (see Illustration 13)
- Tape measure or ruler
- Additional equipment needed to prepare utilization scales:
  - Clipping shears
  - Thread
  - Paper trimmer (for clipping plants into segments)
  - Paper sacks
  - Spring scale calibrated in tenths of grams
  - Graph paper
  - Blank card for utilization gauge

d **Training** This method does not require intensive training for field application, although examiners must be able to identify the plant species. Examiners need to know how to measure and record the height of grazed and ungrazed plants, determine the utilization of individual plants from the gauge, and calculate the average utilization by key species (see Section III.D.9).

e **Establishing Studies** Careful establishment of studies is a critical element in obtaining meaningful data. Select key species and determine the number, length, and location of the transects (see Section III.B.7).

(1) Collect data using several pilot transects to determine the number of transects needed and the number of observations to be made on each transect. These data are needed to determine if a statistically valid sample has been collected (see Section III.B.7).

(2) At the beginning of each study, determine the transect bearing and distance between observation points. Select a prominent distant landmark such as a large tree, rocky point, etc., that can be used as the transect bearing point.

(3) Plot the transects on detailed management unit maps and/or aerial photos (see beginning of Section III).

(4) Permanently mark the location of each study with a reference post and study location stake (see beginning of Section III).

(5) Number studies for proper identification to ensure that the data collected can be positively associated with specific studies on the ground (see Appendix B).

(6) Document the location and other pertinent information concerning the study on the Study Location and Documentation Data form (see beginning of Section III and Appendix A).

f **Sampling Process** Sample ungrazed and grazed plants encountered along a transect to determine the average ungrazed plant height and the average percent utilization. To secure reliable utilization determinations, it is essential to measure heights for an adequate number of ungrazed and grazed plants. The greater the variation in utilization between plants, the more plants required to determine the average utilization.

(1) *Measuring plant heights*

    (a) Best results are obtained by placing the measuring tape or ruler in the center of the bunch or turf circle, rather than along one side. The tape or ruler should not be forced down into the crown but should rest firmly on the cushioned portion of the plant.

    (b) Where rhizomatous/sod-forming grasses or grasslike plants are the key species, use a circle of turf 2 inches in diameter as one plant.

(2) *Sampling plants*

    (a) At each interval along the transect, select the plant of the key species (seedlings excepted) nearest the toe and measure the height of the plant to the nearest 1/4 inch. If plants are not evenly grazed, determine the average stubble height.

    (b) If the selected plant has not been grazed, record the height for that sample in the Ungrazed Height Column on the Height-Weight form (see Illustration 12).

    (c) If the selected plant has been grazed, record the height for that sample in the Grazed Height Column on the Height-Weight form (see Illustration 12)

    (d) Measure at least 20 ungrazed plants to obtain a reliable cross section of ungrazed plant heights. If a sufficient number of ungrazed plants is not encountered along the transect, it may be necessary to extend the transect or add more transects to the baseline (measuring both grazed and ungrazed plants) to pick up the additional ungrazed plant heights. In some cases, it may be necessary to select, in a subjective manner, ungrazed plants on an adjacent area to determine average ungrazed plant height.

(e) Use only one kind of plant. When 80 percent or more of the plants measured produce culms or when 80 percent or more are without culms, the remaining 20 percent or less may be disregarded without great error.

(f) When a combination occurs with 80 percent or more culm-producing plants, and a plant lacking culms is encountered nearest the sampling point, measure the nearest culm-producing plant of the species. Corresponding procedures should be followed when the kind of plant selected is without culms and a culm-producing plant is encountered. These two combinations are those most commonly encountered in the field.

(g) When approximately equal numbers of culm and culmless plants occur, measure plants of both kinds. The measurements for the plants with culms should be marked or kept separate on the form. Be sure to use appropriate ungrazed heights and the correct utilization scales for plants with and without culms.

g **Calculations** Calculate the percent utilization as follows:

(1) Divide the total of the ungrazed plant heights by the number of ungrazed plants sampled to calculate the average ungrazed plant height.

(2) Determine the percent utilization of the key species with the gauge by calculating the average plant heights of all the grazed and ungrazed plants. The sliding card in the gauge is pulled out of the envelope until the utilization scale for the key species appears in the window. The dial is then turned so that the number representing the previously calculated average ungrazed height is set at the arrow designated "Average Ungrazed Height". The percent utilization may then be read on the scale in the window opposite the number on the dial representing the average height of grazed plants. The utilization scale on the sliding card must fit the species being sampled (see Illustration 13). Utilization on individually sampled plants can be calculated by using the measured stubble height instead of the average height of the grazed plants. Use the culmless curve for the key species when seasonal utilization studies are conducted on early growth of the plants.

(3) Calculate the average utilization for a key species by totaling the percent utilization for the individual sampled plants and dividing by the number of sampled plants of that species.

(4) Record the average height of ungrazed plants, percent utilization of individual sampled plants, and average percent utilization for the key species on the Height-Weight form (see Illustration 12).

h **Preparing Utilization Scales** Utilization scales used with the utilization gauge are prepared from height-weight curves developed for individual grass and grasslike species. Previously prepared utilization scales must be checked to see whether or not these scales fit the species on the rangeland where they will be used (See Illustration 13, pages 2, and 3). Where existing utilization scales do not fit, new scales will have to be prepared. Scales for a number of species are included on the same card.

(1) *Developing height-weight curves* Develop height-weight curves by collecting plants of a given species and determining the height—weight relationship for that species. The curve for any given species must be checked for variation between range sites and climatic regions. It is necessary to develop separate curves for culm-producing plants and culmless plants when a species only sporadically produces culms.

(a) Sampling plants. Sample at least ten plants of a given species. Select only those plants which have reached maximum growth.

- At each interval along a pace transect, choose the ungrazed plant of the given species nearest the toe. Use 1 square inch as a unit area for sod-forming species and a comparable number of stems as a unit area for single stem species.

- Remove all old leaves and stems of previous year's growth.

- Clip the plant to within 1/4 inch of the ground.

- Wrap the clipped plant with thread from base to top to retain all leaves and culms in their natural position.

- Separate the plants with culms from plants without culms and consider each as a separate sample.

- Measure heights of clipped plants to the nearest inch and determine the average height.

- Calculate the number of plants that must be sampled to determine average height with a standard error of $\pm$ 3 to 5 percent at the 95 percent confidence level (Barrett and Nutt 1979, Freese 1962).

- Sample additional plants, if necessary.

- Measure the maximum height of each plant.

- Clip the top 10 percent by height of each plant and place the clippings in a paper sack labeled 0 to 10 percent. Clip additional height segments in 10 percent increments and place clippings in appropriately labeled sacks—11 to 20 percent, 21 to 30 percent, 31 to 40 percent, 41 to 50 percent, 51 to 60 percent, 61 to 70 percent, 71 to 80 percent, 81 to 90 percent, and 91 to 100 percent. A large paper trimmer with a guide to hold the plants in their proper position on the platform may be used to clip plants into segments. Label the sacks to show species, date, and location. Place a given height segment for all plants of a species collected in one paper sack.

- Dry the clippings until a final dried weight is achieved. Leave clippings in the paper sacks for drying

(b) Determining height-weight relationships.

- Weigh and record the dry weight for each of the ten height segments to the nearest tenth of a gram. Subtract sack weight before recording the dry weight of each height segment (see Illustration 14).

- Total the dry weight of the ten height segments and record the total dry weight of the collected plants (see Illustration 14).

- Record the cumulative dry weight for each segment. This includes the weight of the segment plus the weights of all preceding segments starting from the top of the plant (see Illustration 14).

- Calculate the cumulative percent height and weight removed at each height segment by dividing the cumulative height or weight for each segment by the total height or weight and multiplying by 100 (see Illustration 14).

- Plot the cumulative percent height removed against the cumulative percent weight removed on graph paper. The resulting curve portrays the height removed-weight removed relationship for the species (see Illustrations 14 and 15).

(2) *Transferring data from curves to scales* Transfer the height-weight relationship data portrayed on the height-weight curve to a utilization scale for use in the utilization gauge. The following text and Illustration 16 present a situation where the average height of ungrazed plants is 10 inches.

(a) Turn the dial on the utilization gauge so that 10 inches is set at the arrow designated "Average Ungrazed Height." With the dial set at 10, each inch increment from 9 to 0 on the dial represents 10 percent of the height (see Illustration 16).

(b) Slide a blank card into the utilization gauge.

(c) Use the height-weight curve to determine the percent height that would be removed when 10 percent, 20 percent, etc., of the weight is removed (see Illustrations 15 and 16).

(d) From the height-weight curve, observe that for 10 percent of the weight to be removed, 46 percent of the height must be removed from the top of the plant. This means that 54 percent of the plant height remains, or 5.4 inches of a 10-inch plant. Find the 5.4-inch point on the circular dial, extend a horizontal line to the blank card, and write a "10" on the card (to show 10 percent utilization). Continue this procedure for 20 percent weight removed, 30 percent weight removed, etc., until all the points are plotted on the card.

(3) ***Documenting scale preparation*** For each utilization scale prepared, maintain a record of the species, the data used to prepare the scale, the date the scale was prepared, and the areas of applicability.

i **Data Analysis** Calculate confidence intervals for both ungrazed and grazed plant heights.

j **References**

Barrett, James P. and Mary E. Nutt. 1979. Survey sampling in the environmental sciences: a computer approach. COMPress, Inc., Wentworth, N.H. 319 p.

Freese, Frank. 1962. Elementary forest sampling. U.S. Dept. of Agr., For. Ser., Agr. Handbook No. 232. 91 p.

Gierisch, Ralph K. 1967. An adaptation of the grazed plant method for estimating utilization of Thurber fescue. J. Range Manage. 20:108-111.

Heady, Harold F. 1950. Studies on bluebunch wheatgrass in Montana and height-weight relationships of certain range grasses. Ecol. Monogr. 20:55-81.

Lommasson, T. and Chandler Jensen. 1938. Grass volume tables for determining range utilization. Science 87:444.

————. 1943. Determining utilization of range grasses from height-weight tables. J. Forestry 41:589-593.

McDougald, Neil K. and Richard C. Platt. 1976. A method of determining utilization for wet mountain meadows on the summit allotment, Sequoia National Forest, California. J. Range Manage. 29:497-501.

National Academy of Sciences/National Research Council. 1962. Basic problems and techniques in range research. NAS/NRC Publ. 890. 341 p.

Pechanec, J.F. and G.D. Pickford. 1937b. A weight-estimate method for the determination of range or pasture production. J. Amer. Soc. Agron. 29:894-904.

U.S. Department of Interior Bureau of Land Management. 1984. Rangeland Monitoring - Utilization Studies, TR4400-3.

Height-Weight

Study Number		Date		Examiner	

Allotment Name & Number	Pasture

Kind and/or Class of Animal	Period of Use

Key Species	Culm		Culmless	

No	Height		% Utilization	No	Height		% Utilization	No	Height		% Utilization	No	Height		% Utilization
	Ungra	Graze			Ungra	Graze			Ungra	Graze			Ungra	Graze	
1				16				31				46			
2				17				32				47			
3				18				33				48			
4				19				34				49			
5				20				35				50			
6				21				36				51			
7				22				37				52			
8				23				38				53			
9				24				39				54			
10				25				40				55			
11				26				41				56			
12				27				42				57			
13				28				43				58			
14				29				44				59			
15				30				45				60			

Number of Ungraz. Plants		Total Height of Ungraz. Plants		Number of Sampled Plants		Total % Util. for All Sampled Plants	

Total Height of Ungrazed Plants / Number of Ungrazed Plants = Average Ungrazed Plant Height	_____ =	Total Percent Utilization / Number of Sampled Plants = Average Utilization	_____ =

Notes (use other side or another page, if necessary)

Illustration 12   95

Height-Weight

Study Number	Date	Examiner
(D-3-21) 8 BAC-1	11/3/95	Jack Frost

Allotment Name & Number	Pasture
Medicine Creek	Spring water

Kind and/or Class of Animal	Period of Use
Cattle	7/1 to 9/30

Key Species	STCO 4	Culm	X	Culmless	

No	Ungra	Graze	% Utilization	No	Ungra	Graze	% Utilization	No	Ungra	Graze	% Utilization	No	Ungra	Graze	% Utilization
1		6	10	16	13		0	31		3	30	46		2	43
2		4	21	17		4	21	32	10		0	47	16		0
3	14		0	18	9		0	33		5	14	48	15		0
4		8	5	19		5	14	34	14		0	49		3	30
5	10		0	20		3	30	35	14		0	50		2	43
6		7	7	21		4	21	36		3	30	51	12		0
7		2	43	22		3	30	37		2	43	52		4	21
8		8	5	23	16		0	38		4	21	53	14		0
9	11		0	24		2	43	39		1	71	54		5	14
10		4	21	25		7	7	40		6	10	55		1	71
11		6	10	26	13		0	41		3	30	56		3	30
12	13		0	27	14		0	42		2	43	57	10		0
13	15		0	28		5	14	43	13		0	58		2	43
14		8	5	29		4	21	44		4	21	59	14		0
15		2	43	30	12		0	45		3	30	60		3	30

Number of Ungraz. Plants	21	Total Height of Ungraz. Plants	272	Number of Sampled Plants	60	Total % Util. for All Sampled Plants	1039

$$\frac{\text{Total Height of Ungrazed Plants}}{\text{Number of Ungrazed Plants}} = \text{Average Ungrazed Plant Height} \qquad \frac{272}{21} = 13$$

$$\frac{\text{Total Percent Utilization}}{\text{Number of Sampled Plants}} = \text{Average Utilization} \qquad \frac{1039}{60} = 17\%$$

Notes (use other side or another page, if necessary)

Utilization Gauge

Front Side of Gauge

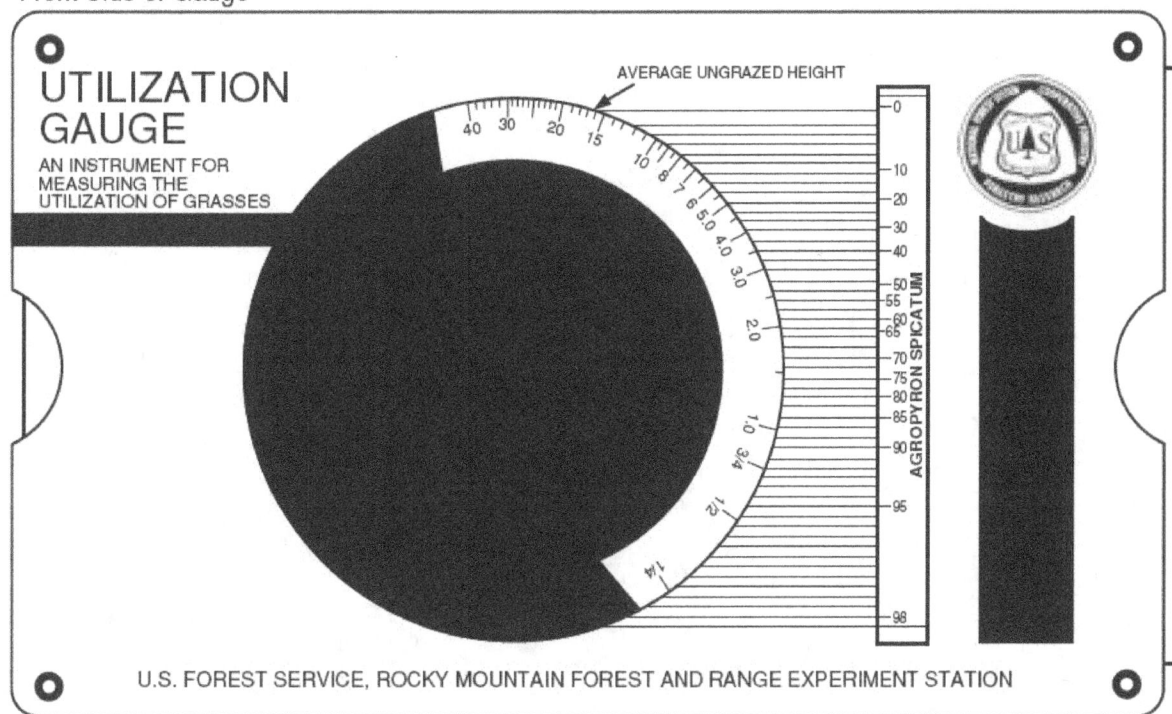

Back Side of Gauge

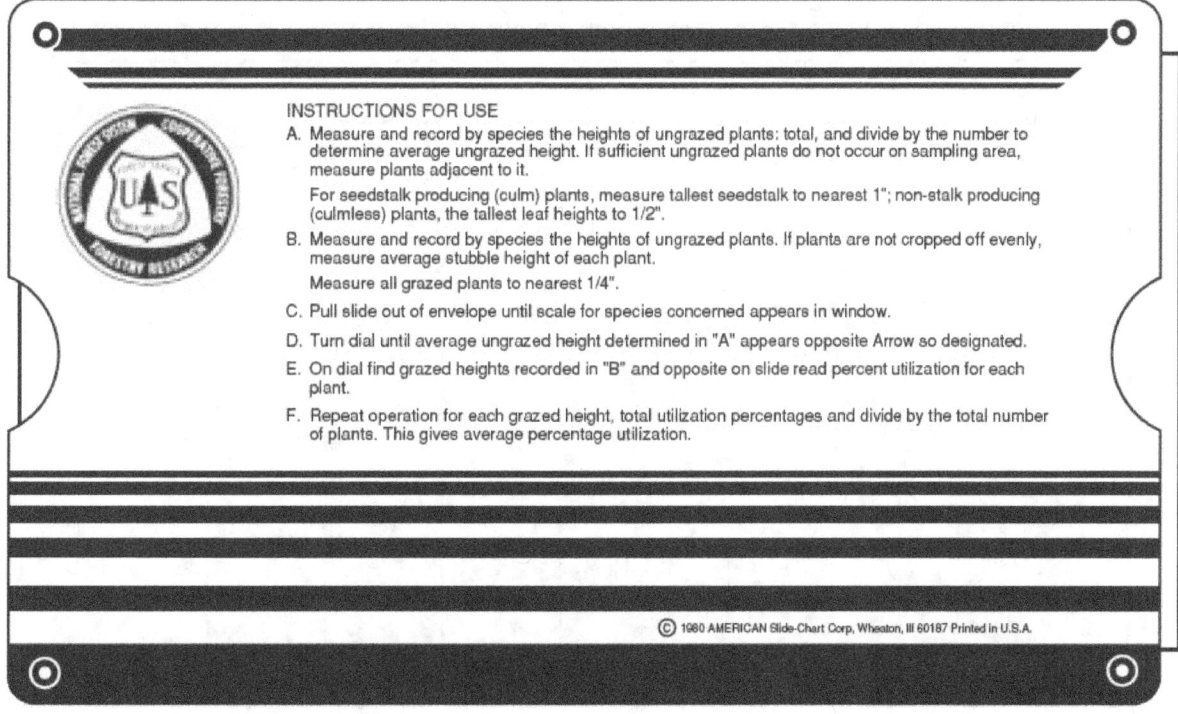

INSTRUCTIONS FOR USE

A. Measure and record by species the heights of ungrazed plants: total, and divide by the number to determine average ungrazed height. If sufficient ungrazed plants do not occur on sampling area, measure plants adjacent to it.

   For seedstalk producing (culm) plants, measure tallest seedstalk to nearest 1"; non-stalk producing (culmless) plants, the tallest leaf heights to 1/2".

B. Measure and record by species the heights of ungrazed plants. If plants are not cropped off evenly, measure average stubble height of each plant.

   Measure all grazed plants to nearest 1/4".

C. Pull slide out of envelope until scale for species concerned appears in window.

D. Turn dial until average ungrazed height determined in "A" appears opposite Arrow so designated.

E. On dial find grazed heights recorded in "B" and opposite on slide read percent utilization for each plant.

F. Repeat operation for each grazed height, total utilization percentages and divide by the total number of plants. This gives average percentage utilization.

© 1980 AMERICAN Slide-Chart Corp, Wheaton, Ill 60187 Printed in U.S.A.

Illustration 13   97

Utilization Gauge (continued)

These utilization scales must be checked to see whether or not they fit the species on the rangeland where they will be used.

Front side of card

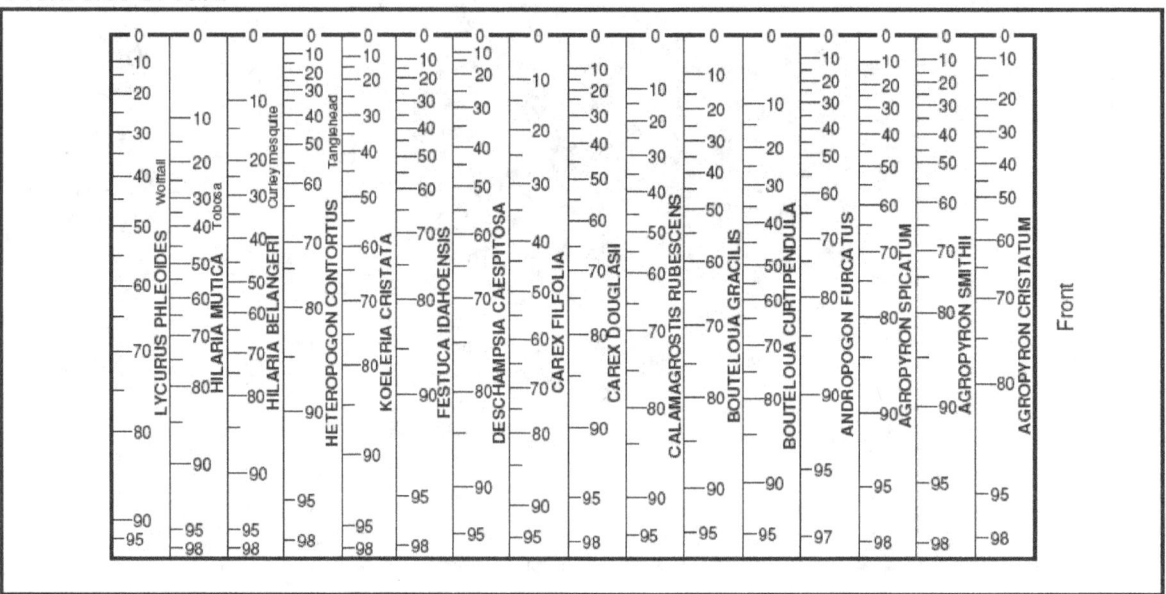

Back side of card

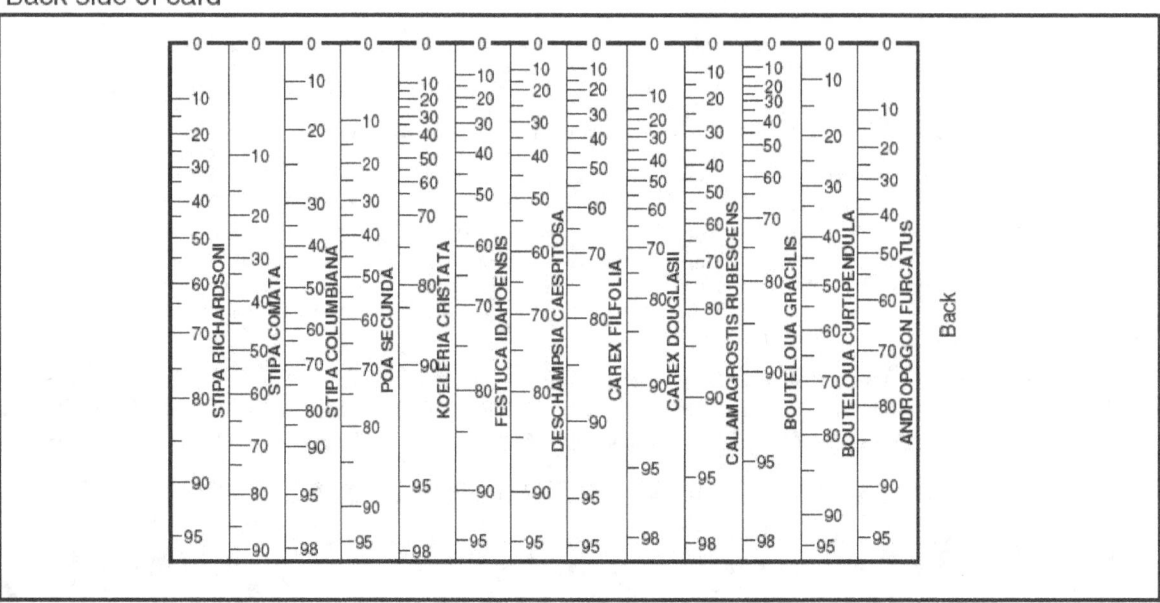

Illustration 13 *page 2*

Utilization Gauge (concluded)

These utilization scales must be checked to see whether or not they fit the species on the rangeland where they will be used.

Front side of card

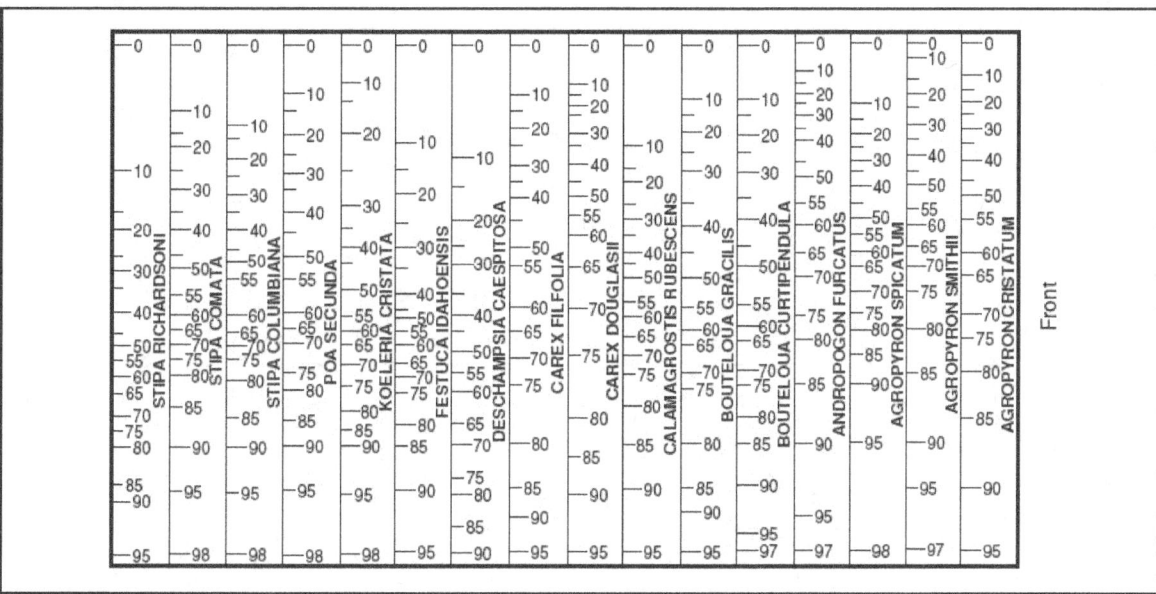

Back side of card

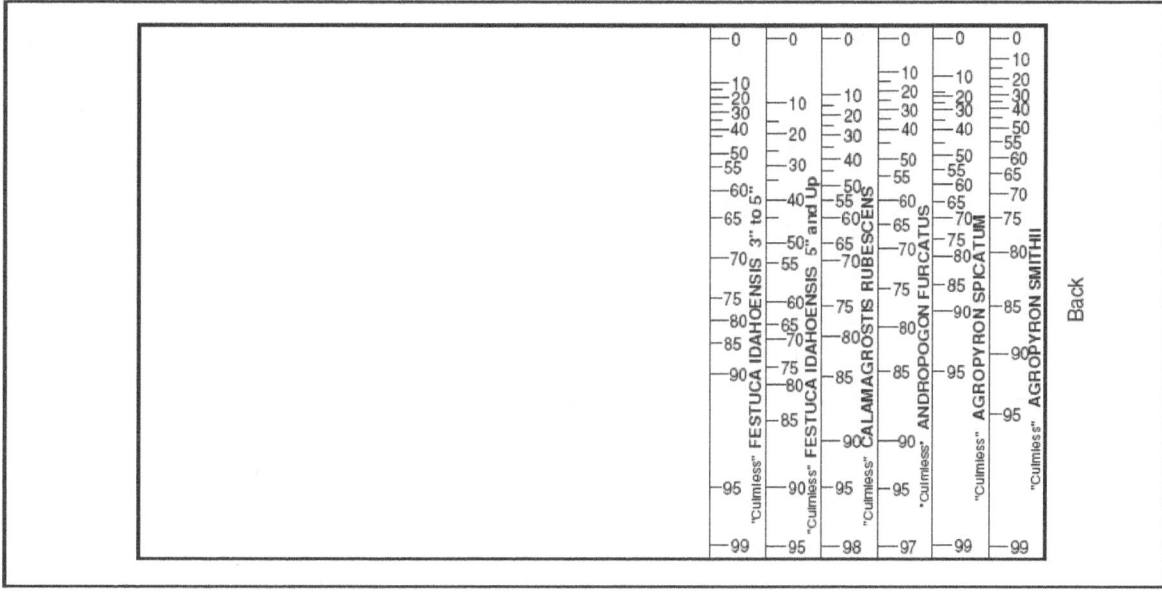

Illustration 13 *page 3*

99

Example of Data Set

Example of Data Set for Determining Height-Weight Relationships Used in Preparing Utilization Scales				
Height Segment (percent)	Dry Weight by Height Segment (grams)	Cumulative Dry Weight (grams)	Cumulative % Height Removed	Cumulative % Weight Removed
0-10	2.8	2.8	10	0.9
11-20	5.6	8.4	20	2.6
21-30	7.0	15.4	30	4.8
31-40	8.4	23.8	40	7.4
41-50	15.4	39.2	50	12.2
51-60	22.1	61.3	60	19.0
61-70	38.3	99.6	70	30.9
71-80	54.6	154.2	80	47.8
81-90	75.7	229.9	90	71.3
91-100	92.6 / 322.5	322.5	100	100.0

Illustration 14

Example of Height-Weight Curve Used for Preparing Utilization Scales

Scientific Name and Code -

Common Name -

Culm Producing or Culmless Plants -

Allotment Name and Number -

Resource Area -

District -

Date -

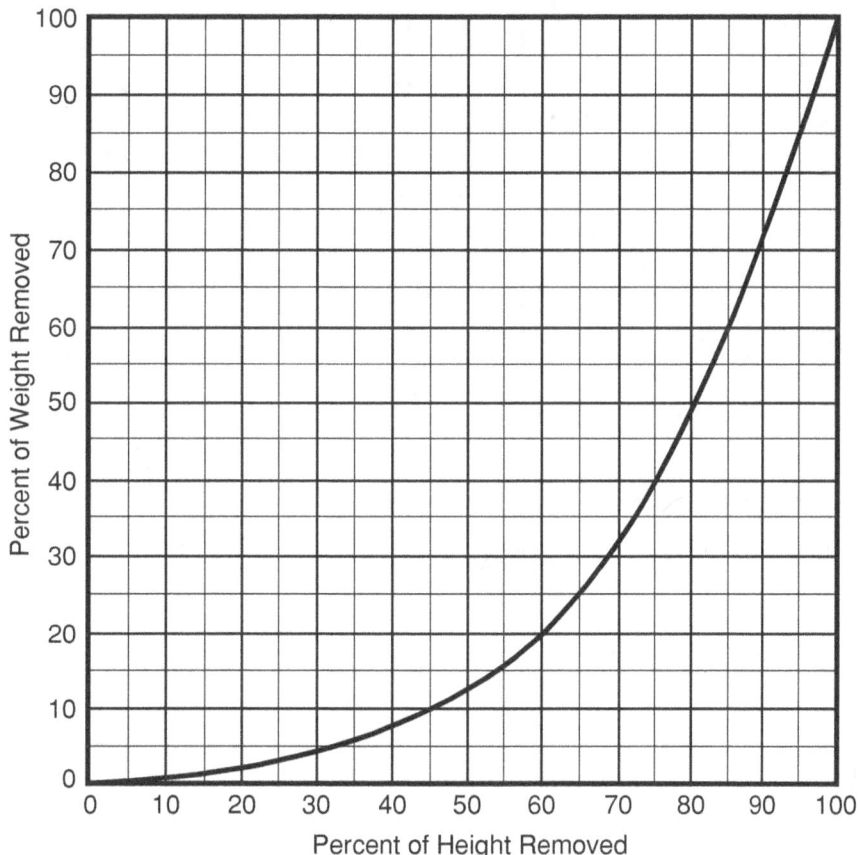

Illustration 15

101

Method for Transferring Data from Height-Weight Curves to Utilization Scales

Scientific Name and Code -

Common Name -

Date -

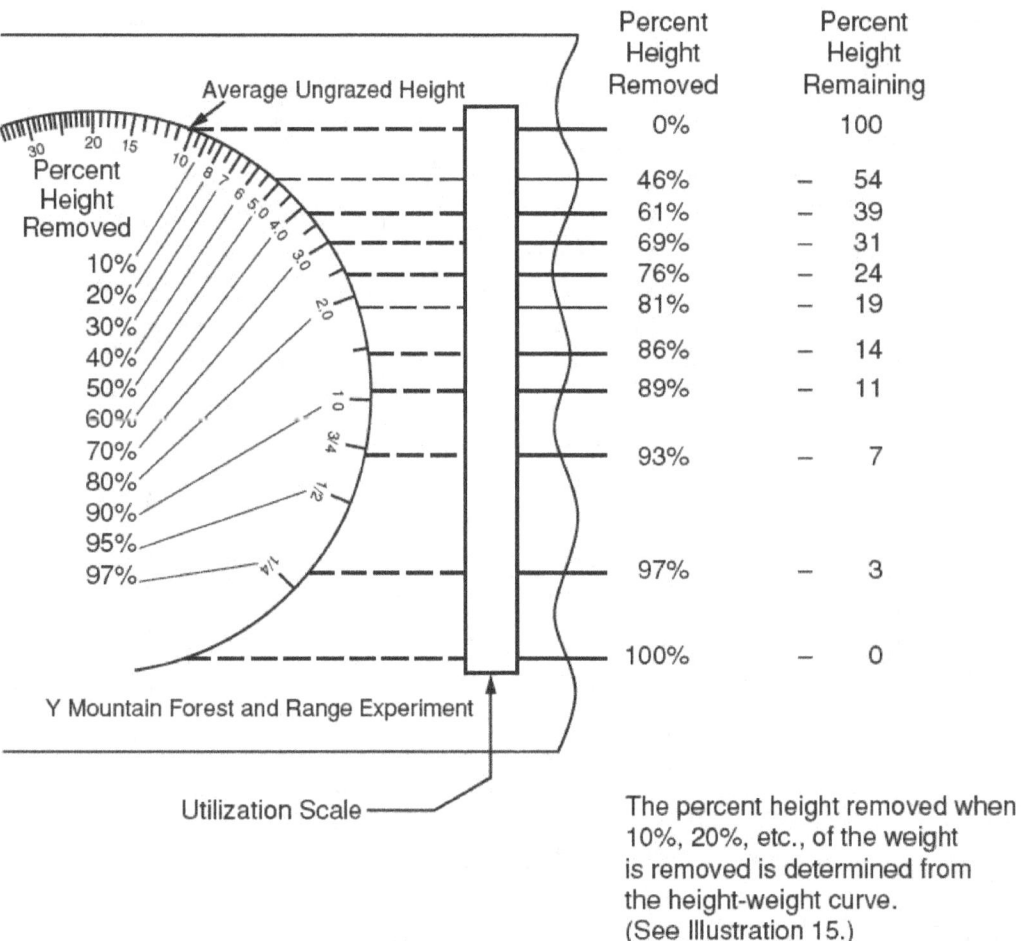

	Percent Height Removed	Percent Height Remaining
	0%	100
	46%	– 54
	61%	– 39
	69%	– 31
	76%	– 24
	81%	– 19
	86%	– 14
	89%	– 11
	93%	– 7
	97%	– 3
	100%	– 0

Average Ungrazed Height

Percent Height Removed
10%
20%
30%
40%
50%
60%
70%
80%
90%
95%
97%

Y Mountain Forest and Range Experiment

Utilization Scale

The percent height removed when 10%, 20%, etc., of the weight is removed is determined from the height-weight curve. (See Illustration 15.)

5. *Actual Weight Method* The Actual Weight Method involves separately clipping and weighing current year's growth from grazed and ungrazed plants along a transect. Only available forage plants are clipped along the transect. The difference between weights represents the amount of forage consumed by animals or otherwise destroyed during the period of use. Where utilization levels are such that few ungrazed plants are available, cages within the pasture or similar reference areas in ungrazed pastures are required to obtain an estimate of the ungrazed weight.

a **Areas of Use** This method is best adapted to clearly defined growth forms such as bunchgrasses. It is not recommended for areas where shrubs or rhizomatous plants are the key species. It can be used on sodforming grasses if a small quadrat, 2 or 3 inches square, is used to delineate a unit.

b **Advantages and Limitations** The method is simple, accurate, and reduces personal error caused by estimation of utilization levels found in other methods. The actual weight method is restricted primarily to bunch and sod-forming grasses. This method is best adapted to short duration grazing on small pastures, which reduces the effects of regrowth.

c **Equipment**

- Study Location and Documentation Data form (see Appendix A)
- Actual Weight form (see Illustration 17)
- Frames to delineate quadrats (if necessary).
- Clipping shears
- Paper sacks
- Spring scale, calibrated in grams
- Cages as required (see Appendix E)

d **Training** Little training is required for this method. Examiners must be able to identify the plant species. Training is limited to clipping and weighing, grazed and ungrazed plants, separating out the current year's growth from residue, and recording the weights.

e **Establishing Studies** Careful establishment of studies is a critical element in obtaining meaningful data. Select key species and determine the number, length, and location of the transects (see Section III.B.7). Place cages within the study site, as required, to obtain a representative sample of the ungrazed weight of all key species.

(1) Collect data using several pilot transects to determine the number of transects needed and the number of observations to be made on each transect. These data are needed to determine if a statistically valid sample has been collected (see Section III.B.7).

(2) At the beginning of each study, determine the transect bearing and distance between observation points. Select a prominent distant landmark such as a large tree, rocky point, etc., that can be used as the transect bearing point.

(3) Plot the transects on detailed management unit maps and/or aerial photos (see beginning of Section III).

(4) Permanently mark the location of each study with a reference post and study location stake (see beginning of Section III).

(5) Number studies for proper identification to ensure that the data collected can be positively associated with specific studies on the ground (see Appendix B).

(6) Document the location and other pertinent information concerning the study on the Study Location and Documentation Data form (see beginning of Section III and Appendix A).

f **Sampling Process** After examiners are trained, proceed with the collection of utilization data.

(1) Select two paper sacks for each key species; one is marked "grazed" and the other "ungrazed."

(2) At each interval along the transect, select the plant of the key species that is nearest the toe and clip it to ground level or some other easily identifiable level. Collection of grazed and ungrazed plants as they occur along the transect is extremely important. Only the plants collected along the transect are used in calculating utilization. Plants clipped from cages or adjoining representative areas (see Section (8) below) used to calculate the average ungrazed weight are not used in the percent utilization calculations.

(3) Place the plant, grazed or ungrazed, in the appropriate sack and mark a tally on the outside of the sack or on a tally sheet. For example, a grazed plant is clipped and placed in the sack marked "grazed". The tally is made so the number of plants in each sack is known.

(4) Clip plants along the transect until there are at least 25 plants (or some other predetermined number) in each of the grazed and ungrazed sacks. Do not discontinue clipping one kind (grazed or ungrazed) of plant when extending the transect to satisfy the minimum quota for the other kind of plant. The grazed and ungrazed sacks will probably not contain the same number of plants. (For example, if the grazed sack contains 25 plants and the ungrazed sack contains 20 plants, continue to clip grazed and ungrazed plants encountered along the transect until the ungrazed sack contains 25 plants. In this example, the grazed sack will probably contain more than 25 plants when the minimum quota of ungrazed plants is finally met.)

(5) Determine the number of grazed and ungrazed plants that were clipped.

(6) Separate out the current year's growth from previous years' residue and then weigh each sack separately to determine the weights of current growth for the grazed and ungrazed plants.

(7) Record the numbers and weights on the Actual Weight form (see Illustration 17).

(8) If enough ungrazed plants cannot be found, clip ungrazed plants from either within the cages placed within the study site, along a transect in an adjoining area, in an ungrazed pasture within the management unit, or in another ungrazed area in the vicinity to obtain the average weight of ungrazed plants. These sites must be as similar as possible (vegetation type, soil, etc.) to the area in which the study is being conducted. It is preferable that dry weight be determined and used in the calculations of percent utilization if an extended period of time will elapse between collection of grazed plants and the collection of ungrazed plants.

g Calculations Calculate the percent utilization as follows:

(1) Step 1. Calculate the average weight of ungrazed plants.

$$\frac{\text{Total weight of ungrazed plants}}{\text{Total number of ungrazed plants}} = \text{Average weight of ungrazed plants}$$

(2) Step 2. Calculate the total weight of all clipped plants as if none had been grazed.

$$\begin{array}{l}\text{Total number of plants clipped along} \\ \text{the transect (both grazed and ungrazed)}\end{array} \text{ x } \begin{array}{l}\text{Average weight} \\ \text{of ungrazed plants}\end{array} = \begin{array}{l}\text{Total weight of all} \\ \text{clipped plants as if} \\ \text{none had been grazed}\end{array}$$

(3) Step 3. Calculate the percent of total production (weight) remaining.

$$\frac{\begin{array}{l}\text{Total weight of clipped plants} \\ \text{(grazed and ungrazed)}\end{array}}{\begin{array}{l}\text{Total weight of all clipped} \\ \text{plants as if none had been grazed}\end{array}} \text{ x } 100 = \text{Percent of total production (weight) remaining}$$

(4) Step 4. Calculate the percent utilized.

$$100\% - \text{Percent of total production (weight) remaining} = \text{Percent utilized}$$

(5) Step 5. Record the percent utilization on the Actual Weight form (see Illustration 17).

h Data Analysis Calculate confidence intervals around the average estimated percent utilization.

i References

Heady, Harold F. 1949. Methods of determining utilization of range forage. J. Range Manage. 2:53-63.

U.S. Department of Interior Bureau of Land Management. 1984. Rangeland Monitoring - Utilization Studies, TR4400-3.

Actual Weight

Study Number	Date	Examiner

Allotment Name & Number	Pasture

Kind and/or Class of Animal	Period of Use

Key Species

Plants	Number of Plants	Total Weight* (grams)
Grazed		
Ungrazed		
Totals		

See other side for explanation of the steps for calculating percent utilization.

Step 1   _____ = Grams per ungrazed plant

Step 2   x   = Grams (weight of all plants as if none had been grazed)

Step 3   _____ x 100 = % of weight remaining

Step 4   100%   −   = % Utilization

Notes (use other side or another page, if necessary)

Key Species

Plants	Number of Plants	Total Weight* (grams)
Grazed		
Ungrazed		
Totals		

See other side for explanation of the steps for calculating percent utilization.

Step 1   _____ = Grams per ungrazed plant

Step 2   x   = Grams (weight of all plants as if none had been grazed)

Step 3   _____ x 100 = % of weight remaining

Step 4   100%   −   = % Utilization

Notes (use other side or another page, if necessary)

* Minus the weight of the sack

Illustration 17

Actual Weight Calculations

Calculate Percent Utilization of Ungrazed Plants as Follows:

Step 1. calculate the average weight of ungrazed plants.

$$\frac{\text{Total weight of ungrazed plants}}{\text{Total number of ungrazed plants}} = \text{Average weight of ungrazed plants}$$

——————————————————— =

Step 2. calculate the total weight of all clipped plants as if none had been grazed.

Total number of plants clipped   x   Average weight of   =   Total weight of all clipped plants
   (both clipped and ungrazed)   ungrazed plants   as if none had been grazed

x =

Step 3. calculate the percent of total production (weight) remaining.

$$\frac{\text{Total weight of clipped plants (grazed and ungrazed)}}{\text{Total weight of all clipped plants as if none had been grazed}} \times 100 = \text{Percent of total production weight remaining}$$

——————————————————— x 100 =

Step 4. calculate the percent utilization.

100% - Percent to total production (weight) remaining   =   Percent utilized

100% - =

Notes:

Illustration 17 *page 2*

107

Actual Weight

Study Number	Date	Examiner
Red Butte	9/19/95	George H. Ruth

Allotment Name & Number	Pasture
Red Butte - 30673	Little Red

Kind and/or Class of Animal	Period of Use
Cattle	6/16 - 9/15

Key Species   FEID

See other side for explanation of the steps for calculating percent utilization.

Plants	Number of Plants	Total Weight* (grams)
Grazed	43	154
Ungrazed	17	142
Totals	60	296

Step 1 $\dfrac{142}{17}$ = 8.4   Grams per ungrazed plant

Step 2   60 x 8.4 = 504   Grams (weight of all plants as if none had been grazed)

Step 3 $\dfrac{296}{504}$ x 100 = 59   % of weight remaining

Step 4   100% - 59 = 41   % Utilization

Notes (use other side or another page, if necessary)

Key Species

See other side for explanation of the steps for calculating percent utilization.

Plants	Number of Plants	Total Weight* (grams)
Grazed		
Ungrazed		
Totals		

Step 1   _____ =   Grams per ungrazed plant

Step 2   x   =   Grams (weight of all plants as if none had been grazed)

Step 3   _____ x 100 =   % of weight remaining

Step 4   100% -   =   % Utilization

Notes (use other side or another page, if necessary)

* Minus the weight of the sack

Illustration 17

6. *Grazed-Class Method* The Grazed-Class Method uses photo guides of key species to make utilization estimates. These estimates reflect herbage removed but also show herbage remaining.

a **Areas of Use** This method is adapted for use on perennial grass, perennial grass-forb, and grass-shrub rangelands where the key species are either bunch or rhizomatous/sod-forming grass or grasslike species. It is designed for use after the plants have achieved full seasonal growth.

b **Advantages and Limitations**

(1) This method is rapid and easy to learn and use. It can be used by livestock operators and examiners to give consistent and accurate estimates of utilization. The mathematics involved are simple.

(2) In poor growth years when plants do not mature, the guides will not distinguish between use and no-growth.

(3) The difficult job is developing photo guides based on average plants on a typical site that have a good photo-height-weight representation. One guide, properly developed for a given species and a typical site, can be used on all sites over a fairly broad area (e.g., the Southwest) in good and bad production years without serious error. The guides serve as standards of comparison that promote consistency in estimates.

(4) The method tends to reduce errors caused by variability in height growth, one of the major sources of error in height-weight methods. In making estimates of utilization by the grazed-class method, the growth form of the plant is used as the primary guide and visual adjustments for differences in height can easily be made by the examiner. (Schmutz et al. 1963)

(5) Another advantage is that, while the estimate of utilization is based on forage removed, each grazed-class shows both the degree of use and the amount of herbage remaining. (Schmutz et al. 1963)

(6) The method facilitates estimation of irregular grazing of plants. Although the guide plants are clipped to a certain height and may not represent the normal pattern of grazing, they do provide a visual picture of the volume by grazed classes and serve as a guide to the examiner in estimating irregular use of the plant, such as occurs in side-trimming of leaves or partial grazing of seed stalks. This requires judgment on the part of the examiner but accuracy increases with experience and errors are off-setting. The method is thus largely free from personal bias yet allows for experienced judgment on grazing use of irregularly grazed plants. (Schmutz et al. 1963)

(7) A minimum of 1 to 2 hours experience by examiners regardless of prior experience will produce uniform accuracy. (Schmutz et al. 1963)

c **Important Considerations**

(1) Errors can be encountered because of variations in plant growth between sites and ecoregions. Photographic guides should therefore be checked

with growth curves of local plants. New guides should be prepared if the existing photo guides do not correspond to the growth curves.

(2) Several guides may need to be developed for each key species to match wide year-to-year or site-to-site variations in growth form. Development of guides based on averages of local plants within a given region will reduce the possibility of variation that might result from using curves developed for broad geographic regions or between states. (Gierisch 1967)

d Equipment

- Study Location and Documentation Data form (see Appendix A)
- Grazed-Class form (see Illustration 18)
- Photo guides (see Illustration 19)
- Tally counter (optional)
- Additional equipment needed to develop photo guides:
  - Clipping shears
  - Paper sacks
  - Spring scale calibrated in tenths of grams
  - Graph paper

e Training
Minimal training of examiners is needed to use this method. Examiners must be able to identify the plant species. The major problem with inexperienced examiners, and examiners who have not used the method for some time, is underestimation of use on more heavily grazed plants.

f Establishing Studies
Careful establishment of studies is a critical element in obtaining meaningful data. Select key species and determine the number, length, and location of the transects (see Section III.B.7).

(1) Collect data using several pilot transects to determine the number of transects needed and the number of observations to be made on each transect. These data are needed to determine if a statistically valid sample has been collected (see Section III.B.7).

(2) At the beginning of each study, determine the transect bearing and distance between observation points. Select a prominent distant landmark such as a large tree, rocky point, etc., that can be used as the transect bearing point.

(3) Plot the transects on detailed management unit maps and/or aerial photos (see beginning of Section III).

(4) Permanently mark the location of each study with a reference post and study location stake (see beginning of Section III).

(5) Number studies for proper identification to ensure that the data collected can be positively associated with specific studies on the ground (see Appendix B).

(6) Document the location and other pertinent information concerning the study on the Study Location and Documentation Data form (see beginning of Section III and Appendix A).

g **Sampling Process**

(1) At each interval along the transect, select the plant(s) of the key species (seedlings excepted) nearest the toe.

(2) Compare the sample plant(s) with the photo guides for that species and classify according to one of six grazed-classes representing 0, 10, 30, 50, 70, or 90 percent use (see Illustration 19).

(3) Base the estimates of utilization on growth form of the plant. Variations in height growth due to site characteristics and seasonal precipitation can be disregarded since variations in height are automatically adjusted for by the eye.

(4) Record the estimates by dot count for each grazed class on the Grazed-Class form (see Illustration 18).

(5) For bunch grasses, make estimates on individual plants.

(6) For rhizomatous/sod-forming key species, make estimates on 6-, 8-, 10-, or 12-inch square quadrats along the transect.

h **Calculations** Calculate the percent utilization as follows:

(1) Convert the dot count to the number of plants sampled by grazed-class.

(2) Multiply the number of plants sampled in each grazed-class by the grazed-class percent.

(3) Total the products for all classes.

(4) Divide the sum by the total number of plants observed on the transect.

(5) Record the average percent utilization on the Grazed-Class form (see Illustration 18).

i **Developing Photo Guides** Photo guides must be developed that have a close relationship between the grazed-class percentages of the guide and the height-weight curve of the plant photographed. Guides are developed as follows:

(1) When plants of a given species have reached full growth, sample 5 to 10 representative plants from a typical site. For bunchy species, sample individual plants. For rhizomatous/sod-forming species, sample plants from a 6-, 8-, 10-, or 12-inch square quadrat.

(2) Beginning at the top of the plant, clip 4- to 10-inch segments from the top portion and 2-inch segments from the lower portion of each plant (see Illustration 20). Place each segment in an individual paper sack. Label the sacks to show species, plant number, segment number, segment length, date, and location. Keep the clippings from each plant separate. Make all height measurements from the base of the plant. For bunchgrasses, use the center of the root crown.

(3) Oven dry and carefully weigh each plant segment to the nearest tenth of a gram. Subtract sack weight before recording the dry weight of each segment (see Illustration 20).

(4) Beginning at the top of the plant, record the cumulative dry weight for each segment. This includes the weight of the segment plus the weights of all preceding segments (see Illustration 20).

(5) Calculate the cumulative percent weight for each segment by dividing the cumulative dry weight for each segment by the total dry weight and multiplying the result by 100 (see Illustration 20).

(6) Beginning at the base of each plant, record the cumulative height remaining by segment. This includes the combined length of all preceding segments (see Illustration 20).

(7) Determine the average height of the clipped plants.

(8) Adjust the height remaining of each individual plant to average plant-height remaining with the following formula:

$$\text{Adjusted individual plant-height remaining} = \frac{\text{Total height of average plant}}{\text{Total height of individual plant}} \times \text{Height remaining of individual plant}$$

(9) Plot the cumulative percent weight of the individual plants against the adjusted individual plant-height remaining on graph paper (see Illustration 21). Use the lower left-hand corner as zero on both scales and plot 5 or 6 clipped plants of a given species on the same graph.

(10) Determine the average plant height for the six grazed-class percentages (percent weight removed), 0, 10, 30, 50, 70 and 90 percent, from the height-weight curves on the graph (see Illustration 21).

(11) Return to the field and select 4 to 6 average plants to be used in making a photo guide for the given species. Use the grazed-class heights read from the average curve on the graph to determine the heights at which to clip the plants to be photographed using the formula:

$$\text{Clipping height of plant to be photographed} = \frac{\text{Total height of plant to be photographed}}{\text{Total height of average plant}} \times \text{Grazed-class height of average plant}$$

(12) Photograph each plant in sequence at the unclipped height and at heights representing 10, 30, 50, 70, and 90 percent of the weight removed. Clip the last increment to ground level or as close as possible. For bunchgrasses, clip to the root crown.

(13) Sack the clippings separately and dry them in an oven. Label the sacks to show species, plant number, clipped height, grazed-class percentage, date, and location.

(14) Determine if the curve of at least one of the photographed plants closely matches the average curve on the graph. In addition, determine if the cumulative weight percentages for the various clipped heights of that plant closely match the grazed-class percentages (within 2 or 3 percentage points). If a close match is obtained, trim the photos and put them on a grazed-class photo guide background (see Illustration 19). If not, repeat the photographing of average plants until a close representation is obtained.

(15) For each photo guide prepared, maintain a record of the species, the data used to prepare the guide, the date the guide was prepared, and the areas of applicability.

j Established Photo Guides The following are sources of existing photo guides.

(1) University of Arizona, Cooperative Extension Service and Agricultural Experiment Station, Tucson Arizona 85721. Bulletin A-73.

(2) University of Idaho, College of Forestry, Wildlife and Range Science, Moscow, Idaho 83843. Station bulletin 54.

(3) Montana State University. Forage Use - A Tool for Planning Range Management. Extension Service. July 1988.

(4) Kinney and Clary. 1994. A Photographic Utilization Guide for Key Riparian Graminoids. USFS GTR-308.

k Data Analysis Calculate confidence intervals around the average Estimated percent utilization.

l References

Gierisch, Ralph K. 1967. An adaptation of the grazed plant method for estimating utilization of Thurber fescue. J. Range Manage. 20:108-111.

Schmutz, Ervin M. 1971. Estimation of range use with grazed-class photo guides. Coop. Extension Service and Agr. Exp. Sta., Univ. of Ariz., Tucson, AZ, Bull. A-73. 16 p.

Schmutz, E.M., G.A. Holt, and C.C. Michaels. 1963. Grazed class method of estimating forage utilization. J. Range Manage. 16:54-60.

U.S. Department of Interior Bureau of Land Management. 1984. Rangeland Monitoring - Utilization Studies, TR4400-3.

Grazed Class

Study Number	Date	Examiner
Allotment Name & Number	Pasture	
Kind and/or Class of Animal	Period of Use	

Grazed Class Percents (P)	Key Species			Key Species			Key Species		
	Dot Count	No by Class (C)	No X Class % (C) (P)	Dot Count	No by Class (C)	No X Class % (C) (P)	Dot Count	No by Class (C)	No X Class % (C) (P)
0									
10									
30									
50									
70									
90									
	Totals			Totals			Totals		

$$\text{avg. util.} = \frac{\Sigma(CP)^*}{\Sigma C}$$ _____ = _____ = _____ =

Notes (Use other side or another page, if necessary)

* Where C = the number of plants within each class (C column), P = the grazed-class percentages (P column), and Σ = the summation symbol.

Grazed Class

Study Number Sandy Arroyo #2	Date 10/26/95	Examiner Mary McCarthy

Allotment Name & Number Sandy Arroyo - 10719	Pasture Creosote Knob

Kind and/or Class of Animal Cattle	Period of Use 8/1 to 10/31

Grazed Class Percents (P)	Key Species BOGR 2			Key Species			Key Species		
	Dot Count	No by Class (C)	No X Class % (C)(P)	Dot Count	No by Class (C)	No X Class % (C)(P)	Dot Count	No by Class (C)	No X Class % (C)(P)
0	⊠ ··	12	0						
10	⊠ ⊓	17	170						
30	⊠⊠⊠:	32	960						
50	⊠ ⊓:	16	800						
70	:·	3	210						
90									
	Totals	80	2140	Totals			Totals		
avg. util. = Σ(CP)*/ΣC	2140/80 = 27%			____ =			____ =		

Notes (Use other side or another page, if necessary)

* Where C = the number of plants within each class (C column), P = the grazed-class percentages (P column), and Σ = the summation symbol.

Illustration 18   115

Grazed Class Method Photo Guides

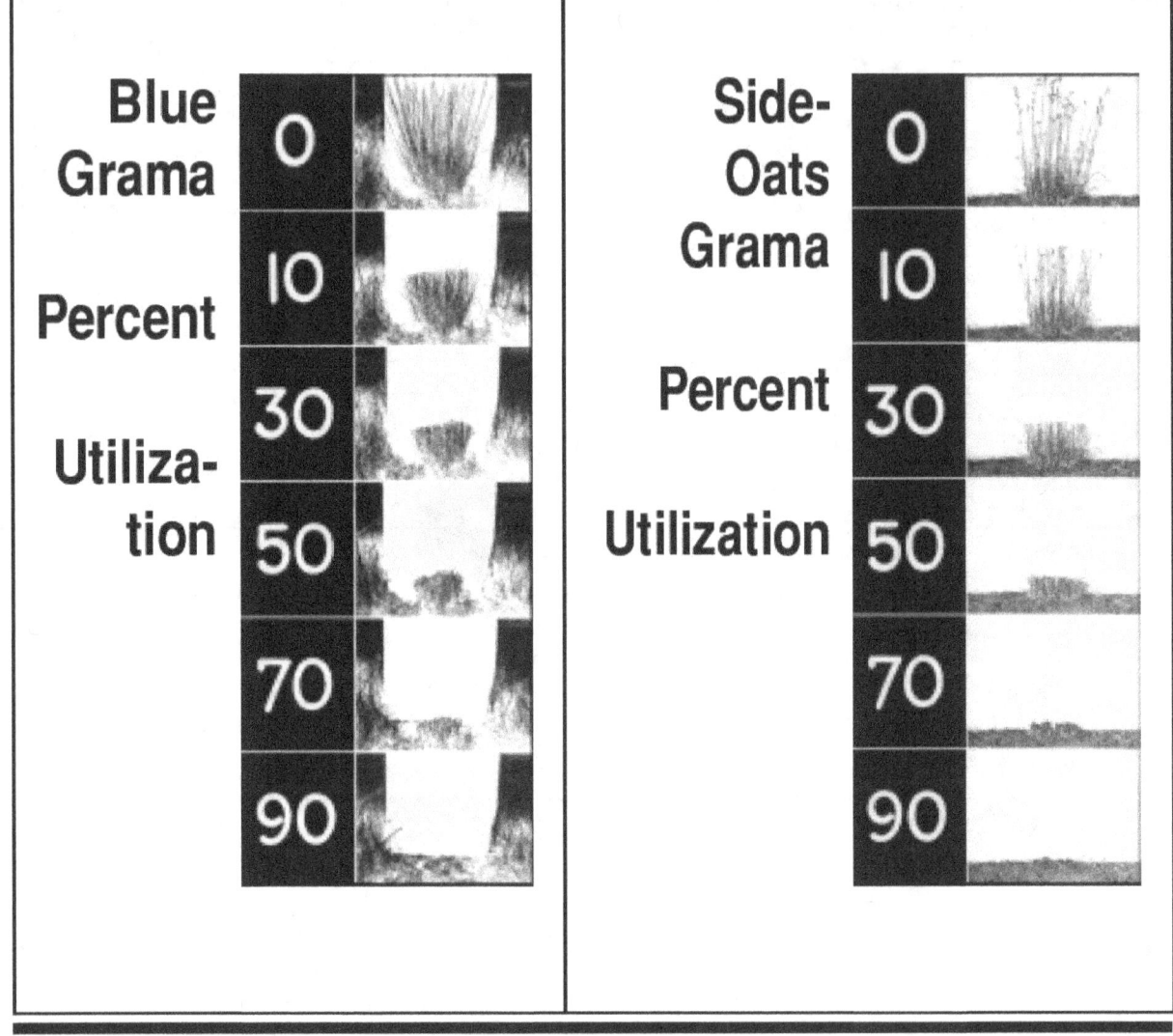

Illustration 19

Example of Data Set for Determining Height-Weight Relationships for Developing Photo Guides

Scientific Name & Code _____

Species _____ Date _____

Segment Number (from top down)	Dry Weight Segment Length (inches)	Cumulative by Plant Segment (grams)	Adjusted Cumulative Dry Weight (grams)	Cumulative Percent Weight	Height Remaining (inches)	Height Remaining (inches)
-	-	-	-	0	21.5	26.0
1	6.5	.9	.9	7.5	15.0	18.1
2	4.0	.9	1.8	15.0	11.0	13.3
3	3.0	.7	2.5	20.8	8.0	9.7
4	2.0	.7	3.2	26.7	6.0	7.3
5	2.0	.9	4.1	34.2	4.0	4.8
6	2.0	1.9	6.0	50.0	2.0	2.4
7	2.0	6.0	12.0	100.000	0	0
	21.5	12.0				

Illustration 20   117

Example of Height-Weight Curve Used for Determining Average Plant Height for the Six Grazed-Class Percentages on Photo Guides

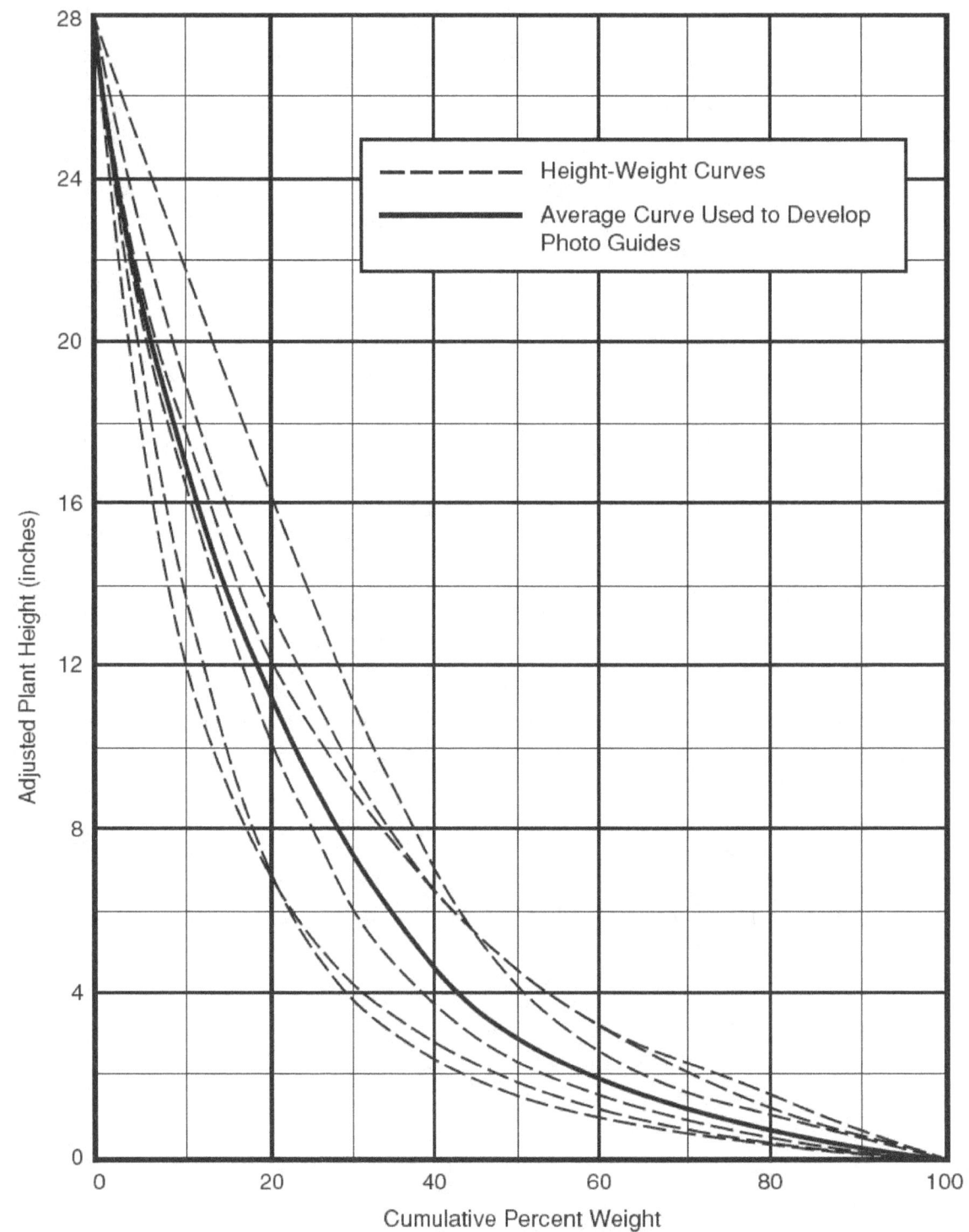

Illustration 21

D. Qualitative Assessments - Landscape Appearance Method (formerly the Key Forage Plant Method)

This technique uses an ocular estimate of forage utilization based on the general appearance of the rangeland. Utilization levels are determined by comparing observations with written descriptions of each utilization class.

a Areas of Use This method is adapted to areas where perennial grasses, forbs, and/or browse plants are present and to situations where utilization data must be obtained over large areas using only a few examiners.

b Advantages and Limitations This method is rapid and does not require unused areas for training purposes. Estimates are based on a range (class) of utilization rather than a precise amount. Different examiners are more likely to estimate utilization in the same classes than to estimate the same utilization percentages. One limitation of this technique is that the method can still result in varying estimates because of different examiners. Another limitation is that there is no way to assess the precision of the estimate because the estimates are qualitative.

c Equipment

- Study Location and Documentation Data form (see Appendix A)
- Landscape Appearance form (see Illustration 22)
- Tally counter (optional)

d Training Personal judgment is involved in any estimation method. Estimates are only as good as the training and experience of the examiners (see Section III.D.9). The training described for the Ocular Estimate and Key Species Methods often helps examiners using this method make the utilization class estimations (see Section V.C.2 and 3). The examiners must be trained to recognize the seven herbaceous or seven browse utilization classes using the written class descriptions. Examiners must think in terms of the general appearance of the rangeland at each observation point, rather than weight or height removed.

e Establishing Studies Careful establishment of studies is a critical element in obtaining meaningful data. Note that it is not necessary to select key species or to complete pilot studies, since statistical analysis is not possible under this method.

(1) At the beginning of each study, determine the transect bearing and distance between observation points. Select a prominent distant landmark such as a large tree, rocky point, etc., that can be used as the transect bearing point.

(2) Plot the transects on detailed management unit maps and/or aerial photos (see beginning of Section III).

(3) Permanently mark the location of each study with a reference post and study location stake (see beginning of Section III).

(4) Number studies for proper identification to ensure that the data collected can be positively associated with specific studies on the ground (see Appendix B).

(5) Document the location and other pertinent information concerning the study on the Study Location and Documentation Data form (see beginning of Section III and Appendix A).

f **Sampling Process** After examiners are trained and have confidence in their ability to judge utilization by utilization classes, proceed with the collection of utilization data. At each observation point along the transect, estimate the utilization class using the written description of the classes. In those cases where part of a class description does not apply (example: percentage of seedstalks remaining), judge utilization based on those parts of the description that do apply. An observation point is the immediate area visible to examiners when standing at a particular location along the transect. Record the estimates by dot count by utilization class on the Landscape Appearance From (see Illustration 22).

(1) *Herbaceous utilization classes* Seven utilization classes are used to show relative degrees of use of herbaceous species (grasses and forbs). Each class represents a numerical range of percent utilization. Estimate utilization within one of the seven classes. Utilization classes are as follows:

(a) (0-5%). The rangeland shows no evidence of grazing use or negligible use.

(b) (6-20%). The rangeland has the appearance of very light grazing. The herbaceous forage plants may be topped or slightly used. Current seedstalks and young plants are little disturbed.

(c) (21-40%). The rangeland may be topped, skimmed, or grazed in patches. The low value herbaceous plants are ungrazed and 60 to 80 percent of the number of current seedstalks of herbaceous plants remain intact. Most young plants are undamaged.

(d) (41-60%). The rangeland appears entirely covered as uniformly as natural features and facilities will allow. Fifteen to 25 percent of the number of current seedstalks of herbaceous species remain intact. No more than 10 percent of the number of low-value herbaceous forage plants are utilized. (Moderate use does not imply proper use.)

(e) (61-80%). The rangeland has the appearance of complete search. Herbaceous species are almost completely utilized, with less than 10 percent of the current seedstalks remaining. Shoots of rhizomatous grasses are missing. More than 10 percent of the number of low-value herbaceous forage plants have been utilized.

(f) (81-94). The rangeland has a mown appearance and there are indications of repeated coverage. There is no evidence of reproduction or current seedstalks of herbaceous species. Herbaceous forage species are completely utilized. The remaining stubble of preferred grasses is grazed to the soil surface.

(g) (95-100). The rangeland appears to have been completely utilized. More than 50 percent of the low-value herbaceous plants have been utilized.

(2) **Browse utilization classes** Seven utilization classes show relative degrees of use of available current year's growth (leaders) of browse plants (shrubs, half shrubs, woody vines, and trees). Each class represents a numerical range of percent utilization. Estimate utilization within one of the seven classes. Utilization classes are as follows:

(a) (0-5%). Browse plants show no evidence of grazing use or only negligible use.

(b) (6-20%). Browse plants have the appearance of very light use. The available leaders of browse plants are little disturbed.

(c) (21-40%). There is obvious evidence of leader use. The available leaders appear cropped or browsed in patches and 60 to 80% of the available leader growth of browse plants remains intact.

(d) (41-60%). Browse plants appear rather uniformly utilized and 40 to 60% of the available leader growth of browse plants remains intact.

(e) (61-80%). The use of the browse gives the appearance of complete search. The preferred browse plants are hedged and some plant clumps may be slightly broken. Nearly all available leaders are used and few terminal buds remain on browse plants. Between 20 and 40% of the available leader growth of browse plants remains intact.

(f) (81-94%). There are indications of repeated coverage. There is no evidence of terminal buds and usually less than 20% of available leader growth on browse plants remains intact. Some patches of second and third years' growth may be grazed. Hedging is readily apparent and the browse plants are more frequently broken. Repeated use at this level will produce a definitely hedged or armored growth form.

(g) (95-100). Less than 5% of the available leader growth on browse plants remains intact. Some, and often much, of the more accessible second and third years' growth of the browse plants has been utilized. All browse plants have major portions broken.

g Calculations Calculate the percent utilization as follows:

(1) Convert the dot count to the number of observations for each utilization class.

(2) Multiply the number of observations in each utilization class times the midpoints of the class intervals.

(3) Total the products for all classes.

(4) Divide the sum by the total number of observations on the transect.

(5) Record the average percent utilization on the Landscape Appearance form (see Illustration 22).

h Data Analysis Calculate confidence intervals around average estimated percent utilization.

i References

Anderson, E. William and Wilbur F. Currier. 1973. Evaluating zones of utilization. J. Range Manage. 26:87-91.

Heady, Harold F. 1949. Methods of determining utilization of range forage. J. Range Manage. 2:53-63.

U.S. Department of Interior Bureau of Land Management. 1984. Rangeland Monitoring - Utilization Studies, TR4400-3.

Landscape Appearance

Study Number		Date	Examiner

Allotment Name & Number		Pasture

Kind and/or Class of Animal	Period of Use

Class Interval	Int Mid (M)	Dot Count	No. By Class (C)	No. X Midmt. (C)(M)	
0-5%	2.5				(a) (0-5%). The rangeland shows no evidence of grazing or negligible use.
6-20%	13				(b) (6-20%). The rangeland has the appearance of very light grazing. The herbaceous forage plants may be topped or slightly used. Current seedstalks and young plants are little disturbed.
21-40%	30				(c) (21-40%). The rangeland may be topped, skimmed, or grazed in patches. The low value herbaceous plants are ungrazed and 60 to 80 percent of the number of current seedstalks of herbaceous plants remain intact. Most young plants are undamaged.
41-60%	50				(d) (41-60%). The rangeland appears entirely covered as uniformly as natural features and facilities will allow. Fifteen to 25 percent of the number of current seedstalks of herbaceous species remain intact. No more than 10 percent of the number of low-value herbaceous forage plants are utilized. (Moderate use does not imply proper use.)
61-80%	70				(e) (61-80%). The rangeland has the appearance of complete search. Herbaceous species are almost completely utilized, with less than 10 percent of the current seedstalks remaining. Shoots of rhizomatous grasses are missing. More than 10 percent of the number of low-value herbaceous forage plants have been utilized.
81-94%	88				
95-100%	97.5				(f) (81-94). The rangeland has a mown appearance and there are indications of repeated coverage. There is no evidence of reproduction or current seedstalks of herbaceous species. Herbaceous forage species are completely utilized. The remaining stubble of preferred grasses is grazed to the soil surface.
		Totals			

$$\text{Avg. Util.} = \frac{\Sigma(CM)^*}{\Sigma C} \qquad \underline{\hspace{4cm}} =$$

(g) (95-100). The rangeland appears to have been completely utilized. More than 50 percent of the low-value herbaceous plants have been utilized.

Notes (use other side or another page, if necessary)

* Where C = The number of observations within each class interval (C column),
M = the class interval midpoint (M column),
and Σ = the summation symbol.

Illustration 22　　　123

Browse Utilization Classes

(a) (0-5%). Browse plants show no evidence of use; or only negligible use.

(b) (6-20%). Browse plants have the appearance of very light use. The available leaders of browse plants are little disturbed.

(c) (21-40%). There is obvious evidence of leader use. The available leaders appear cropped or browsed in patches and 60 to 80% of the available leader growth of browse plants remains intact.

(d) (41-60%). Browse plants appear rather uniformly utilized and 40 to 60% of the available leader growth of browse plants remains intact.

(e) (61-80%). The use of the browse gives the appearance of complete search. The preferred browse plants are hedged and some plant clumps may be slightly broken. Nearly all available leaders are used and few terminal buds remain on browse plants. Between 20 and 40% of the available leader growth of browse plants remains intact.

(f) (81-94%). There are indications of repeated coverage. There is no evidence of terminal buds and usually less than 20% of available leader growth on browse plants remains intact. Some patches of second and third years' growth may be grazed. Hedging is readily apparent and the browse plants are more frequently broken. Repeated use at this level will produce a definitely hedged or armored growth form.

(g) (95-100). Less than 5% of the available leader growth on browse plants remains intact. Some, and often much, of the more accessible second and third years' growth of the browse plants has been utilized. All browse plants have major portions broken.

Illustration 22 *page 2*

Landscape Appearance

Study Number	Date	Examiner
13N - 41E - 27 - 04	9-29-95	Walter Johson

Allotment Name & Number	Pasture
Blue Ridge - 70079	Chokecherry

Kind and/or Class of Animal	Period of Use
Cattle	5/1 - 9/30

Class Interval	Int Mid (M)	Dot Count	No. By Class (C)	No. X Midmt. (C)(M)
0-5%	2.5		6	15
6-20%	13		13	169
21-40%	30		16	480
41-60%	50		32	1600
61-80%	70		10	700
81-94%	88		3	264
95-100%	97.5		0	
		Totals	80	3228

$$\text{Avg. Util.} = \frac{\Sigma(CM)^*}{\Sigma C} \qquad \frac{3228}{80} = 40.35$$

(a) (0-5%). The rangeland shows no evidence of grazing or negligible use.

(b) (6-20%). The rangeland has the appearance of very light grazing. The herbaceous forage plants may be topped or slightly used. Current seedstalks and young plants are little disturbed.

(c) (21-40%). The rangeland may be topped, skimmed, or grazed in patches. The low value herbaceous plants are ungrazed and 60 to 80 percent of the number of current seedstalks of herbaceous plants remain intact. Most young plants are undamaged.

(d) (41-60%). The rangeland appears entirely covered as uniformly as natural features and facilities will allow. Fifteen to 25 percent of the number of current seedstalks of herbaceous species remain intact. No more than 10 percent of the number of low-value herbaceous forage plants are utilized. (Moderate use does not imply proper use.)

(e) (61-80%). The rangeland has the appearance of complete search. Herbaceous species are almost completely utilized, with less than 10 percent of the current seedstalks remaining. Shoots of rhizomatous grasses are missing. More than 10 percent of the number of low-value herbaceous forage plants have been utilized.

(f) (81-94). The rangeland has a mown appearance and there are indications of repeated coverage. There is no evidence of reproduction or current seedstalks of herbaceous species. Herbaceous forage species are completely utilized. The remaining stubble of preferred grasses is grazed to the soil surface.

(g) (95-100). The rangeland appears to have been completely utilized. More than 50 percent of the low-value herbaceous plants have been utilized.

Notes (use other side or another page, if necessary)

* Where C = The number of observations within each class interval (C column),
M = the class interval midpoint (M column),
and Σ = the summation symbol.

Illustration 22   125

E. Other Methods

1. *Stem Count* This technique is used by very few field offices. It will be moved to BLM's *Rangeland Inventory and Monitoring Supplemental Studies*, Technical Reference 4400-5.

2. *Herbage Capacitance Meter* Capacitance meters have been used to determine utilization level by assessing the weight of standing vegetation. Since this procedure is not widely used on arid rangelands, it will not be addressed here. Additional information on using capacitance meters can be obtained in the following references:

   Currie, P.O., M.J. Morris, and D.L. Neal. 1973. Uses and capabilities of electronic capacitance instruments for estimating standing herbage. Part 2. Sown ranges. J. BR. Grassl. Soc 28:155-160.

   Morris, M.J., K.L. Johnson, and D.L. Neal. 1976. Sampling shrub ranges with electronic capacitance instruments, J. Range Manage. 29:78-81.

   Neal Donald L., and J.L. Neal. 1973. Uses and capabilities of electronic capacitance instruments for estimating standing herbage. Part 1. History and Development. J. Br. Grassl Soc. 28:81-89

   Neal, Donald L., P.O. Currie and M.J.Morris. 1976. Sampling herbaceous vegetation with electronic capacitance instruments, J. Range Manage. 29:74-77.

VI. GLOSSARY OF TERMS

A

actual use: a report of the actual livestock grazing use certified to be accurate by the permittee or lessee. Actual use may be expressed in terms of animal unit months or animal months.

allotment: an area of land designated and managed for grazing of livestock. Such an area may include intermingled private, State, or Federal lands used for grazing in conjunction with the public lands.

allotment management plan (AMP): a documented program which applies to livestock grazing on the public lands, prepared by consultating, cooperating, and coordinating with the permittee(s), lessee(s), or other involved affected interests.

analysis: (1) a detailed examination of anything complex in order to understand its nature or determine its essential features; or (2) a separating or breaking up of any whole into its component parts for the purpose of examining their nature, function, relationship, etc. (A rangeland analysis includes an examination of both biotic (plants, and animals) and abiotic (soils, topography, etc.) attributes of the rangeland.)

annual plant: a plant that completes its life cycle and dies in 1 year or less.

animal month: a month's tenure upon the rangeland by one animal. Animal month is not synonymous with animal unit month.

animal unit: considered to be one mature cow of approximately 1,000 pounds, either dry or with calf up to 6 months of age, or their equivalent, based on a standardized amount of forage consumed.

animal unit month (AUM): the amount of dry forage required by one animal unit for one month based on a forage allowance of 26 pounds per day.

available forage: that portion of the forage production that is accessible for use by a specified kind or class of grazing animal.

B

biomass: the total amount of living plants and animals above and below ground in an area at a given time.

browse: (1) the part of shrubs, half shrubs, woody vines, and trees available for animal consumption; or (2) to search for or consume browse.

browse plant or browse species: a shrub, half shrub, woody vine, or tree capable of producing shoot, twig, and leaf growth suitable for animal consumption.

C

canopy cover: the percentage of ground covered by a vertical projection of the outermost perimeter of the natural spread of foliage of plants. Small openings within the canopy are included. Canopy cover is synonymous with crown cover.

class of livestock: the age and/or sex groups of a kind of livestock.

community: an assemblage of populations of plants and/or animals in a common spatial arrangement.

composition: the proportions (percentages) of various plant species in relation to the total on a given area. It may be expressed in terms of relative cover, relative density, relative weight, etc.

cool season species: Plants whose major growth occurs during the late fall, winter, and early spring.

critical area: An area which should be treated with special consideration because of inherent site factors, size, location, condition, values, or significant potential conflicts among uses.

crown cover: (See canopy cover.)

D

density: numbers of individuals or stems per unit area. (Density does not equate to any kind of cover measurement.)

E

ecological site: a kind of rangeland with a specific potential natural community and specific physical site characteristics, differing from other kinds of rangeland in its ability to produce vegetation and to respond to management. Ecological sites are defined and described with soil, species composition, and production emphasis. Ecological site is synonymous with range site and ecological types (FS).

ecological status: the present state of vegetation of an ecological site in relation to the potential natural community for the site. Ecological status is independent of use. It is an expression of the relative degree to which the kinds, proportions, and amounts of plants in a community resemble that of the potential natural community. The four ecological status classes correspond to 0-25, 26-50, 51-75, or 76-100 percent similarity to the potential natural community and are called *early seral, mid seral, late seral,* and *potential natural community,* respectively.

estimated use: the use made of forage on an area by wildlife, wild horses, wild burros, and/ or livestock where actual use data are not available. Estimated use may be expressed in terms of animal unit months or animal months.

evaluation: (1) an examination and judgment concerning the worth, quality, significance, amount, degree, or condition of something; or (2) the systematic process for determining the effectiveness of on-the-ground management actions and assessing progress toward meeting management objectives.

F

forage: (1) browse and herbage which is available and can provide food for animals or be harvested for feeding; or (2) to search for or consume forage.

forage production: the weight of forage that is produced within a designated period of time or on a given area. Production may be expressed as green, air dry, or oven dry weight. The term may also be modified as to time of production such as annual, current year, or seasonal forage production.

forb: (1) any herbaceous plant other than those in the Poaceae (true grasses), Cyperaceae (sedges), and Juncaceae (rushes) families—i.e., any nongrass-like plant having little or no woody material on it; or (2) a broadleaved flowering plant whose above-ground stem does not become woody and persistent.

forestland: land on which the vegetation is dominated by trees. Lands are classified forestland if the trees now present will provide 25 percent or greater canopy cover at maturity. Lands not presently forestland that were originally or could become forested through natural succession may be classified as potential natural forestland.

frequency: a quantitative expression of the presence or absence of individuals of a species in a population. It is defined as the percentage of occurrence of a species in a series of samples of uniform size.

G

goal: the desired state or condition that a resource management policy or program is designed to achieve. A goal is usually not quantifiable and may not have a specific date by which it is to be completed. Goals are the base from which objectives are developed. (See objective.)

grass: any plant of the family Gramineae.

grassland: land on which the vegetation is dominated by grasses, grasslike plants, and/or forbs. Non-forested lands are classified as grassland if herbaceous vegetation provides at least 80 percent of the canopy cover, excluding trees. Lands not presently grassland that were originally or could become grassland through natural succession may be classified as potential natural grassland.

grasslike plant: a plant of the Cyperaceae or Juncaceae families which vegetatively resembles a true grass of the Gramineae family.

ground cover: The percentage of material, other than bare ground covering the land surface. It may include live and standing dead vegetation, litter cobble, gravel, stones, and bedrock. Ground cover plus bare ground would total 100 percent.

H

half shrub: a plant with a woody base whose annually produced stems die each year.

herbaceous: vegetation growth with little or no woody component; nonwoody vegetation such as graminoids and forbs.

hedging: (1) the appearance of browse plants that have been browsed so as to appear artificially clipped; or (2) consistent browsing of terminal buds of browse species that results in excessive lateral branching and a reduction in upward and outward growth.

herbage: the above-ground material of any herbaceous plant (grasses and forbs).

I

interpretation: explaining or telling the meaning of something and presenting it in understandable terms.

inventory: the systematic acquisition and analysis of information needed to describe, characterize, or quantify resources for land-use planning and management of the public lands.

K

key area: a relatively small portion of a rangeland selected, based on its location, use, or grazing value, as a monitoring for grazing use. It is assumed that key areas, if properly selected, will reflect the overall acceptability of current grazing management over the range.

key species: (1) forage species whose use serves as an indicator to the degree of use of associated species. (2) those, species which must, because of their importance, be considered in a management program.

kind of livestock: species of domestic livestock—cattle, sheep, horses, burros, and goats.

M

monitoring: the orderly collection, analysis, and interpretation of resource data to evaluate progress toward meeting management objectives.

0

objective: planned results to be achieved within a stated time period. Objectives are subordinate to goals, are narrower and shorter in range, and have increased possibility of attainment. Time periods for completion and the outputs or achievements that are measurable and quantifiable, are specified. (See goal.)

overstory: The upper canopy or canopies of plants, usually referring to trees, shrubs, and vines.

P

pasture: grazing area enclosed and separated from other areas by fence or natural barrier.

plant association: a kind of potential natural community consisting of stands with essentially the same dominant species in corresponding layers.

potential natural community (PNC): the biotic community that would become established if all successional sequences were completed without interferences by human beings under the present environmental conditions. Natural disturbances are inherent in development. PNC can include naturalized non-native species.

proper use: (1) a degree of utilization of current year's growth which, if continued, will achieve management objectives and maintain or improve the long-term productivity of the site; or (2) the percentage a plant is utilized when the rangeland as a whole is properly utilized. Proper use varies with time and systems of grazing. Proper use is synonymous with proper utilization.

proper utilization: (See proper use.)

public lands: any land and interest in land outside of Alaska owned by the United States and administered by the Secretary of the Interior through the Bureau of Land Management (See 43 CFR 4100.0-5.)

R

rangeland: a kind of land on which the native vegetation is predominantly grasses, grass-like plants, forbs, or shrubs; includes lands revegetated naturally or artificially when routine management of that vegetation is through manipulation of grazing. Rangelands include natural grasslands, savannas, shrublands, most deserts, tundra, alpine communities, coastal marshes, and wet meadows. Rangelands also include lands revegetated naturally or artificially to provide a plant cover that is managed like native vegetation.

range site: (See ecological site.)

riparian zone: the banks and adjacent areas of water bodies, water courses, seeps, and springs whose waters provide soil moisture sufficiently in excess of that otherwise available locally so as to provide a more moist habitat than that of contiguous flood plains and uplands.

S

savanna: a grassland with scattered trees, whether as individuals or clumps; often a transitional type between true grassland and forest.

seral community: one of a series of biotic communities that follow one another in time on any given area. Seral community is synonymous with successional community.

seral stage: the developmental stages of an ecological succession. Seral stage is synonymous with successional stage.

shrub: a plant that has persistent woody stems and a relatively low growth habit, and that generally produces several basal shoots instead of a single bole. It differs from a tree by its low stature—less than 5 meters (16 feet)—and nonarborescent form.

shrubland: land on which the vegetation is dominated by shrubs. Nonforested lands are classified as shrubland if shrubs provide more than 20 percent of the canopy cover, excluding trees. Lands not presently shrubland that were originally or could become shrubland through natural succession may be classified as potential natural shrubland.

stratification: subdividing an area into units which are, more or less, internally homogeneous with respect to those characteristics of interest.

stubble: The basal portion of herbaceous plants remaining after the top portion has been harvested either artificially or by grazing animals.

succession: the orderly process of community change; it is the sequence of communities which replace one another in a given area.

successional community: (See seral community.)

successional stage: (See seral stage.)

T

tree: a woody perennial, usually single-stemmed plant that has a definite crown shape and characteristically reaches a mature height of at least 5 meters (16 feet). Some plants, such as oaks (Quercus spp.), may grow as either trees or shrubs.

trend: the direction of change in ecological status or in resource value ratings observed over time. Trend in ecological status is described as "toward" or "away from" the potential natural community or as "not apparent." Appropriate terms are used to describe trends in resource value ratings. Trends in resource value ratings for several uses on the same site at a given time may be in different directions, and there is no necessary correlation between trends in resource value ratings and the trend in ecological status.

U

understory: plants growing beneath the canopy of other plants. Usually refers to grasses, forbs, and low shrubs under a tree or shrub canopy.

unsuitable rangeland: rangeland which has no potential value for, or which should not be used for, a specific use because of permanent physical or biological restrictions. When unsuitable rangeland is identified, the identification must specify what use or uses are unsuitable (e.g., "unsuitable for cattle grazing").

use: (See utilization.)

useable forage: that portion of the forage that can be grazed without damage to the basic resources; may vary with season of use, species, and associated species.

utilization: the proportion or degree of the current year's forage production that is consumed or destroyed by animals (including insects). The term may refer either to a single plant species, a group of species, or to the vegetation community as a whole. Utilization is synonymous with use.

V

vegetation: plants in general, or the sum total of the plant life above and below ground in an area.

vegetation type: a kind of existing plant community with distinguishable characteristics described in terms of the present vegetation that dominates the aspect or physiognomy of the area.

vigor: relates to the relative robustness of a plant in comparison to other individuals of the same species. It is reflected primarily by the size of a plant and its parts in relation to its age and the environment in which it is growing.

W

warm season species: plants whose major growth occurs during the spring, summer, or fall and that are usually dormant in winter.

wet meadow: a meadow where the surface remains wet or moist throughout the summer, usually characterized by sedges and rushes.

VII. REFERENCES

Anderson, E. William and Wilbur F. Currier. 1973. Evaluating zones of utilization. J. Range Manage. 26:87-91.

Barrett, James P. and Mary E. Nutt. 1979. Survey sampling in the environmental sciences: a computer approach. COMPress, Inc., Wentworth, NH. 319 p.

Currie, P.O., M.J. Morris, and D.L. Neal. 1973. Uses and capabilities of electronic capacitance instruments for estimating standing herbage. Part 2. Sown ranges. J. BR. Grassl. Soc 28:155-160.

Ferguson, Robert B. and Michael A. Marsden. 1977. Estimating overwinter bitterbrush utilization from twig diameter-length-weight relations. J. Range Manage. 30:231-236.

Freese, Frank. 1962. Elementary forest sampling. U.S. Dept. of Agr., For. Ser., Agr. Handbook No. 232. 91 p.

Frischknecht, Neil C. and Paul W. Conrad. 1965. Adaptable, transportable utilization cages. J. Range Manage. 18:33-34.

Gierisch, Ralph K. 1967. An adaptation of the grazed plant method for estimating utilization of Thurber fescue. J. Range Manage. 20:108-111.

Grieg-Smith, P. 1983. Quantitative plant ecology. 3rd Ed. University of California Press Berkeley and Las Angeles. 359p.

Hansen, Herbert C. 1962. Dictionary of ecology. Bonanza Books, Crown Publishers, Inc., New York, NY. 382 p.

Harniss, Roy 0. and Robert B. Murray. 1976. Reducing bias in dry leaf weight estimates of big sagebrush. J. Range Manage. 29:430-432.

Hart, R.H. 1980. Determining a proper stocking rate for a grazing system. In: Proceedings, Grazing Management Systems for South West Rangelands Symposium, Range Improvement Task Force, New Mexico State Univ., Las Cruces, NM. p. 49-64.

Heady, Harold F. 1949. Methods of determining utilization of range forage. J. Range Manage. 2:53-63.

————. 1950. Studies on bluebunch wheatgrass in Montana and height-weight relationships of certain range grasses. Ecol. Monogr. 20:55-81.

Hewitt, George B., Ellis W. Huddleston, Robert J. Lavigne, Darrell N. Ueckert, and J. Gordon Watts. 1974. Rangeland entomology. Society for Range Management, Range Science Series No. 2. 127 p.

Hooper, Jack F. and Harold F. Heady. 1970. An economic analysis of optimum rates of grazing in the California annual-type grassland. J. Range Manage. 23:307-311.

Hurd, Richard M. and N.A. Kissinger. 1953. Estimating utilization of Idaho fescue (Festuca idahoensis) on cattle range by percent of plants grazed. U.S. Dept. of Agr., For. Ser., Rocky Mtn. For. and Range Exp. Sta., Ft. Collins, CO, Research Paper. 12.

Hurd, Richard. 1959. Factors influencing herbage weight of Idaho fescue plants. J. Range Manage. 12:61-63.

Jasmer, Gerald E. and Jerry Holechek. 1984. Determining Grazing Intensity on Rangelands. Journal of Soil and Water Conservation. 25(5):346-352

Jensen, Charles H. and George W. Scotter. 1977. A comparison of twiglength and browsed-twig methods of determining browse utilization. J. Range Manage. 30:64-67.

Jones, M.B. and R.A. Evans. 1959. Modification of the step-point method for evaluating species yield changes in fertilizer trials on annual grasslands. Agron. J. 51:467-470.

Kinney, John W. and Warren P. Clary. 1994. A Photographic Guide for key Riparian Graminoids. Intermountain For. and Range Exp. Sta., Ogden, Ut. 14p .

Krebs, C.J. 1989. Ecological methodology. Harper & Row, New York, NY.

Lillesand, Thomas M. and Ralph Kiefer. 1979. Remote sensing and image interpretation. John Wiley and Sons, New York, NY. 612 p.

Lommasson, T. and Chandler Jensen. 1938. Grass volume tables for determining range utilization. Science 87:444.

————. 1943. Determining utilization of range grasses from height-weight tables. J. Forestry 41:589-593.

McDougald, Neil K. and Richard C. Platt. 1976. A method of determining utilization for wet mountain meadows on the summit allotment, Sequoia National Forest, California. J. Range Manage. 29:497-501.

McQuisten, Richard and Karl A. Gebhardt. 1983. Analytical reliability in the decision making process—the numbers game. J. Range Manage. 36:126-128.

Meyer, Merle, Fred Batson, and Duane Whitmer. 1982. Helicopter-borne 35mm aerial photography applications to range and riparian studies. IAFHE RSL Res. Rep. 82-1, Coll. of Forestry and Agricultural Experiment Station, Univ. of Minn., St. Paul, MN. 80 p.

Meyer, Merle and Phillip Grumstrup. 1978. Operating manual for the 35mm aerial photography system, 2nd Rev. IAFHE RSL Res. Rep. 78-1, Coll. of Forestry, Univ. of Minn., St. Paul, MN. 62 p.

Milne, A. 1959. The centric systematic area-sample treated as a random sample. Biometrics 15:270-297.

Morris, M.J., K.L. Johnson, and D.L. Neal. 1976. Sampling shrub ranges with electronic capacitance instruments, J. Range Manage. 29:78-81.

Mueller-Dombois, Dieter and Heinz Ellenberg. 1974. Aims and methods of vegetation ecology. John Wiley & Sons, New York, NY. 547 p.

Mueggler, W.F. 1976. Number of plots required for measuring productivity of mountain grasslands in Montana. U.S. Dept. of Agr., For. Ser., Res. Note INT-207. Intermountain For. and Range Exp. Sta., Ogden, UT. 6 p.

Myers, Wayne L. and Ronald L. Shelton. 1980. Survey methods for ecosystem management. A Wiley-Interscience Publication, John Wiley & Sons, New York, NY. 403 p.

National Academy of Sciences/National Research Council. 1962. Basic problems and techniques in range research. NAS/NRC Publ. 890. 341 p.

Neal Donald L. and J.L. Neal. 1973. Uses and capabilities of electronic capacitance instruments for estimating standing herbage. Part 1. History and Development. J. Br. Grassl Soc. 28:81-89

Neal, Donald L., P.O. Currie, and M.J.Morris. 1976. Sampling herbaceous vegetation with electronic capacitance instruments, J. Range Manage. 29:74-77.

Nie, Norman H., C. Hadlai Hull, Jean G. Jenkins, Karin Steinbrenner, and Dale H. Bent. 1975. Statistical package for the social sciences, SPSS. 2nd Ed. McGraw-Hill Book Co., New York, NY. 675 p.

Odum, Eugene P. 1971. Fundamentals of ecology. 3rd Ed. W.B. Saunders Co., Philadelphia, PA. 547 p.

Oosting, Henry J. 1956. The study of plant communities—an introduction to plant ecology. 2nd Ed. W.H. Freeman and Co., San Francisco, CA. 440 p.

Pechanec, J.F. 1936. Comments on the stem-count method of determining utilization of ranges. Ecology 17:329-331.

Pechanec, J.F. and G.D. Pickford. 1937a. A comparison of some methods used in determining percentage utilization of range grasses. J. Agr. Res. 54:753-765.

————. 1937b. A weight-estimate method for the determination of range or pasture production. J. Amer. Soc. Agron. 29:894-904.

Pechanec, J.F. and George Stewart. 1949. Grazing spring-fall sheep ranges of southern Idaho. U.S. Dept. of Agr., Circular No. 808. 34 p.

Phillips, E.A. 1959. Methods of vegetation study. Holt, Rinehart, and Winston, Inc., New York, NY. 107 p.

Reid, E.H. and G.D. Pickford. 1941. A comparison of the ocular-estimate by-plot and the stubble-height methods for determining percentage utilization of range grasses. J. Forestry 39:935-941.

Richardson, Arlo E. 1981. Report on the feasibility of using phenoclimatography models to predict range development and production on BLM winter ranges. BLM Contract No. UT-910-CTO-003. 73 p.

REFERENCES

Richardson, Arlo E. and Stephen G. Leonard. 1981. Climatic modeling of winter rangelands in Utah. In: Ext. Abstract 15th Conf. on Agr. and For. Meteorology and 5th Conf.
on Eiometeorology. Anaheim, CA. p. 182-185.

Roach, M.E. 1950. Estimating perennial grass utilization on semi-desert cattle ranges by
percentage of ungrazed plants. J. Range Manage. 3:182-185.

Robel, R.J., J.N. Briggs, A.D. Dayton, and L.C. Hulbert. 1970. Relationships Between Visual
Obstruction Measurements and Weight of Grassland Vegetation, J. Range Manage.
23:295.

Robel, R.J. 1970. Possible Role of Behavior in Regulating Greater Prairie Chickens'
Populations, J. Wildlife Manage. Vol 34 (2).

Rossiter, R.C. 1966. Ecology of the Mediterranean annual-type pasture. Advances in
Agronomy 18:1-56.

Sampson, Arthur W. 1952. Range management - principles and practices. John Wiley and
Sons, New York, NY. 570 p.

Schaeffer, R.L., W. Mendenhall, and L. Ott. 1979. Elementary survey sampling. Duxbury
Press, North Scituate, MA.

Schmutz, Ervin M. 1971. Estimation of range use with grazed-class photo guides. Coop.
Ext. Ser. and Agr. Exp. Sta., Univ. of Ariz., Tucson, AZ. Bull. A-73. 16 p.

————. 1978. Let's put manage in range management. Rangeman's Journal 5:185-188.

Schmutz, E.M., G.A. Holt, and C.C. Michaels. 1963. Grazed class method of estimating
forage utilization. J. Range Manage. 16:54-60.

Schultz, Arnold M., Robert P. Gibbens, and Leonard DeBano. 1961. Artificial populations
for teaching and testing range techniques. J. Range Manage. 14:236-242.

Schwartz, Chas. C., Edward C. Thor, and Gary H. Elsner. 1976. Wildlands planning glossary.
U.S. Dept. of Agr., For. Ser., Pacific Southwest For. and Range Exp. Sta., Berkeley, CA.,
Gen. Tech. Rept. PSW-13. 252 p.

Sharp, Lee, Kenneth Sanders, and Neil Rimby. 1994. Management decisions based on
utilization - Is it really management? Rangeland 16:38-40.

Smith, A.D. 1944. A study of the reliability of range vegetation estimates. Ecology 25:441-448.

————. 1965. Determining common use grazing capacities by application of the key
species concept. J. Range Manage. 18:196-201.

Smith, Arthur D. and Philip J. Urness. 1962. Analyses of the Twig Length Method of
determining utilization of browse. Utah State Dept. of Fish & Game. Publication No.
62-9. 35p.

Snedecor, George W. and William C. Cochran. 1989. Statistical methods. 8th Ed. Iowa
State University Press, Ames, IA. 503 p.

Snyder, W.D. 1991. Wheat stubble as nesting cover for ring necked pheasants in northern Colorado. Wildlife Soc. bulletin vol 19(4).

Society for Range Management. 1974. A glossary of terms used in range management. 2nd Ed. M.M. Kothmann (ed.), SRM Publ. 36 p.

————. 1975. Rangeland reference areas. William A. Laycock (ed.), SRM Publ., Range Science Series, No. 3. 66 p.

————. 1983. Guidelines and terminology for range inventories and monitoring. Report of the Range Inventory Standardization Committee. 13 p.

Steel, Robert G.D. and James H. Torrie. 1980. Principles and procedures of statistics. 2nd Ed. McGraw-Hill Book Co., Inc., New York, NY. 633 p.

Stickney, Peter F. 1966. Browse utilization based on percentage of twig numbers browsed. J. Wildl. Manage. 30:204-206.

Stoddart, Laurence A., Arthur D. Smith, and Thadis W. Box. 1975. Range management. 3rd Ed. McGraw-Hill Book Co., New York, NY. 532 p.

Vallentine, John F. 1990. Grazing management. Academic Pres Inc, San Diego, CA. 533 p.

USDA Forest Service. 1962. Range Research Methods a Symposium. Misc Publication No. 940. 1962. 172p.

USDA, Forest Service. 1994. Rangeland Analysis and Management Training Guide, Rocky Mountain Region USDA Forest Service, Denver, CO.

U.S. Department of Interior Bureau of Land Management. 1984. Rangeland Monitoring - Utilization Studies, TR4400-3.

Williams, B. 1978. A sampler on sampling. John Wiley & Sons, New York, NY.

Zar, Jerrold H. 1984. Biostatistical analysis. 2nd Ed. Prentice-Hall, Inc., Englewood Cliffs, NJ. 718 p.

APPENDIX A

Study Location and Documentation Data Form

Study Location & Documentation Data

Study Method	Study Number

Allotment Name & Number	Pasture

District	Resource Area

Ecological Site	Plant Community

Date Established	Established by (Name)	Map Reference

Elevation	Slope	Exposure	Aerial Photo Reference

Township	Range	Section	1/4	1/4	1/4

Scale: ____ inches equals one mile

Location

Key Species				

1   2   3

Distance and bearing between reference post or reference point and the transect location stake, beginning of transect, or plot				

Distance and bearing between location stake and bearing stake

Transect Bearing	Vertical Distance Between Ground & Aligned Tape

Length of Transect	Plot/Frame Size

Sampling Interval	Total Number of Samples

Notes (Description of study location, diagram of transect/plot layout, description of photo points, etc. If more space is needed, use reverse side or another page.)

Note: Depending on the study method, fill in the blocks that apply when a study is established. This documentation enables the examiners to conduct follow-up studies in a consistant manner to provide comparable data for analysis, interpretation, and evaluation.

Study Location & Documentation Data

Study Method *Key Species Utilization*	Study Number *035-27W-08-03*

Allotment Name & Number *Quaking Aspen - 11037*	Pasture *Sheep Creek*

District *Howe*	Resource Area *Lost Mountain*

Ecological Site *Clayey-15-19" Northern Plains*	Plant Community *ARTR 2 - AGSP - PONE 3*

Date Established *7/24/95*	Established by (Name) *Charlie Wagon*	Map Reference *Graystone 7½ min. topo*

Elevation *4300*	Slope *Flat*	Exposure *East*	Aerial Photo Reference *BLM-24CN-A277A- 4/22/78*

Township	Range	Section	1/4	1/4	1/4	
3 S	*27W*	*8*	*NW*	*SE*	*NW*	Scale: *2* inches equals one mile

Location

Key Species				
		×		
1 *AGSP* 2 3				

Distance and bearing between reference post or reference point and the transect location stake, beginning of transect, or plot			

Distance and bearing between location stake and bearing stake

Transect Bearing *25° - Toward Highest Point of Skyline*	Vertical Distance Between Ground & Aligned Tape
Length of Transect	Plot/Frame Size

Sampling Interval *Every 5 paces*	Total Number of Samples *50*

Notes (Description of study location, diagram of transect/plot layout, description of photo points, etc. If more space is needed, use reverse side or another page.)

This study is located approximately 1 mile North of the Antelope Draw Spring Development.

Note: Depending on the study method, fill in the blocks that apply when a study is established. This documentation enables the examiners to conduct follow-up studies in a consistant manner to provide comparable data for analysis, interpretation, and evaluation.

APPENDIX B—STUDY IDENTIFICATION

A. Numbering Studies Studies should be numbered to assure positive identification. These numbers can also be used to identify photographs. Following are three alternative schemes for numbering studies:

1. *Numbering Scheme 1.* Consecutive numbers may be assigned to studies within an allotment. For example, Mooncreek #1 and Mooncreek #2 would be studies Number 1 and 2 within the Mooncreek Allotment. A disadvantage to using the names of allotments in a numbering scheme is that these names can, and often do, change.

2. *Numbering Scheme 2.* Studies may be numbered based on their location within a township, range, and section. A 10-character number can be assigned in the following manner:

    a The first three characters are the township (03S), the second three are the range (27W), the next two are the section (08), and the last two are simply a series number (01) assigned to a study based on the number of studies located within a section.

    b The numbers for studies located in Section 8 would be 03S-27W-08-01, 03S-27W-08-02, and so forth.

    c Depending on the local situation, this scheme can be modified by adding characters to the code where there are fractional townships or ranges, where there are more than 99 sections/tracts within a township, and/or where there is more than one public land survey principal meridian and baseline within the area of jurisdiction.

3. *Numbering Scheme 3.* Studies may be numbered based on their location relative to the initial point of survey (principal meridian and baseline governing public land survey).

    a Under this scheme, the first character is a letter assigned to a principal meridian and baseline quadrant. Using the initial point of the survey as the center point, the northeast quadrant (townships located to the north and east of the initial point) is coded "A". The northwest, southwest, and southeast quadrants are coded "B", "C", and "D", respectively. For example:

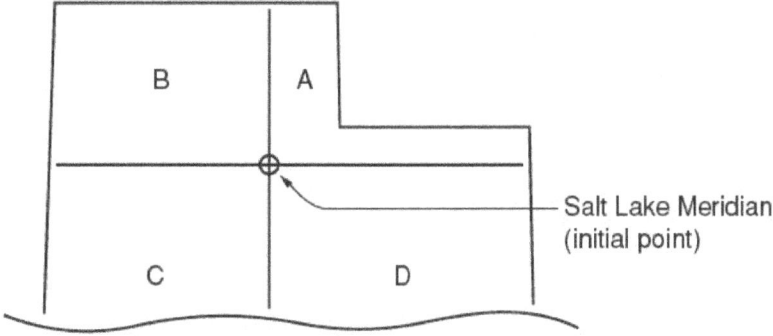

b The next characters are the township number (3, 16, etc.) followed by the range number (7, 32, etc.) and the section number (8, 21, etc.).

c The next three characters are used to identify the subdivisions within a section (down to 10 acres) in which a study is located. These subdivisions have letter designations as follows:

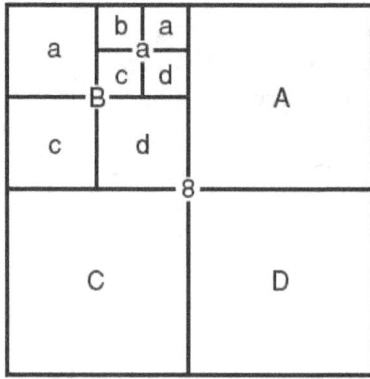

d The last character(s) is (are) simply a series number (1, 2, 3, . . . 10, 11, etc.) assigned to a study based on the number of studies located within the smallest subdivision.

e For example, Studies 1 and 2 located in the SE1/4NE1/4NW1/4 of Section 8, T3S, R21E would be numbered (D-3-21)8Bad-1 and (D-3-21)8Bad-2.

f Depending on the local situation, this scheme can be modified by adding characters to the code where there are fractional townships or ranges, where there are more than 99 sections/tracts within a township, and/or where there is more than one public land survey principal meridian and baseline within the area of jurisdiction.

APPENDIX C

Transect Schematic

Transect Schematic
Technique for Selecting the Nearest Plant

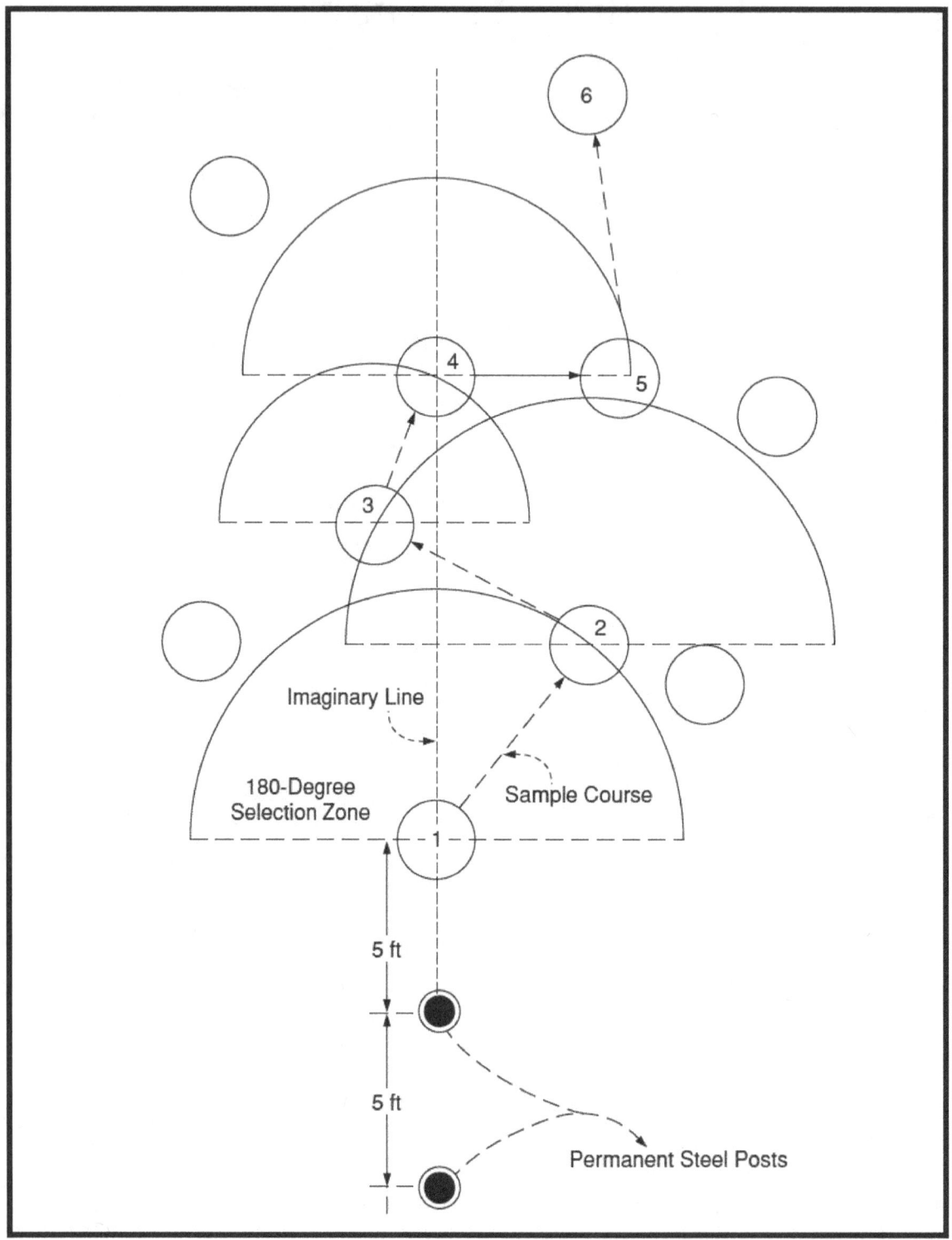

APPENDIX D

Degrees of Hedging

Degrees of Hedging

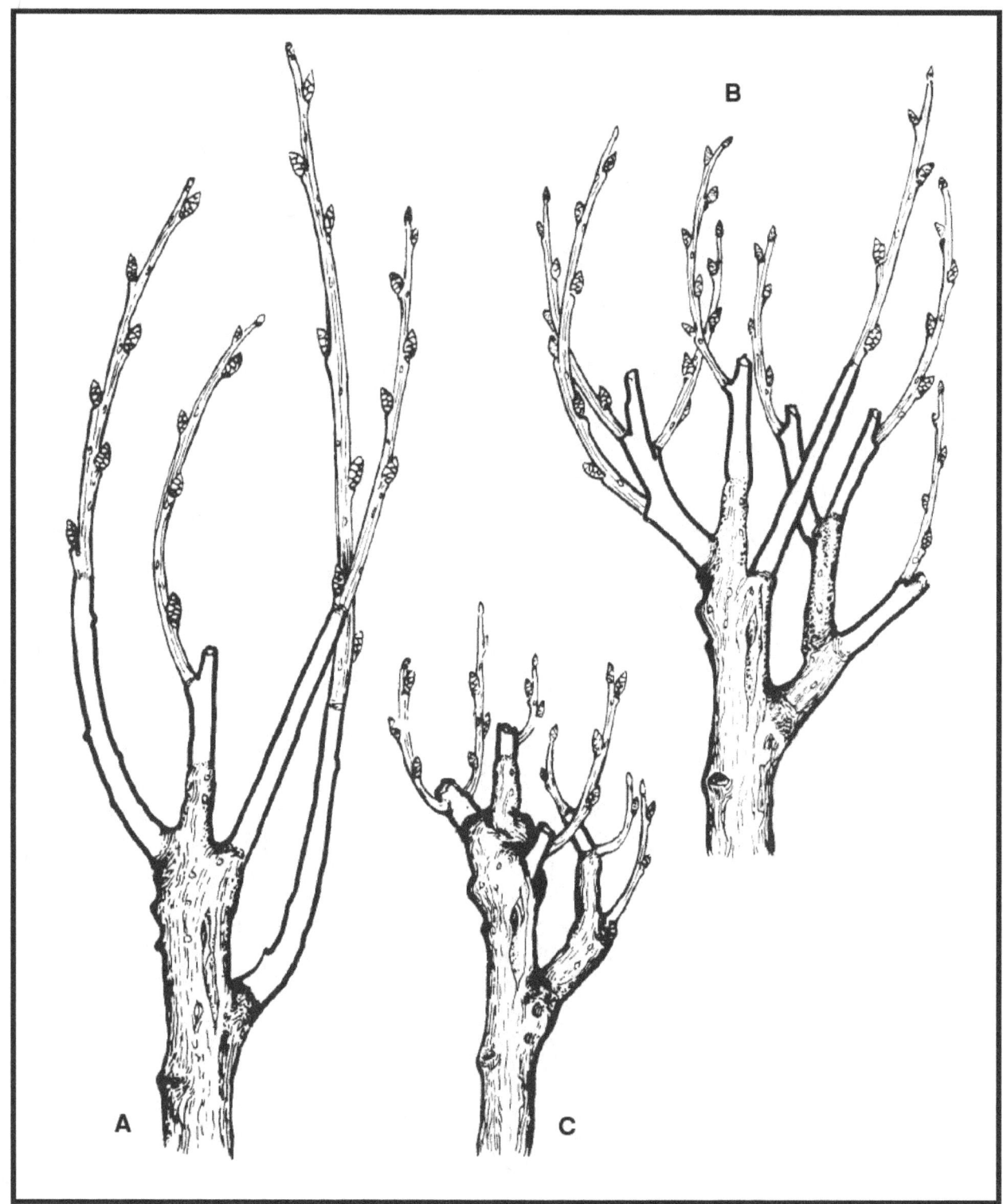

A = Zero to Light   B = Moderate   C = Severe

APPENDIX E

Utilization Cages

Following are some examples of kinds of cages that can be constructed and used for utilization and production studies. There are many other kinds of cages that will do the job just as well. No specific cage is recommended.

Cage Type 1

Folding cages are adaptable to plots of different sizes. The basic construction employs panels of welded wire, hinged together by No. 9 wire threaded through a series of wire loops at the edges of each panel. The 4-sided cage constitutes the basic design, but the number of panels can be increased to enclose larger areas. A 4-panel cage that is 5 feet square accommodates a 9.6 sq. ft. plot, 5 panels accommodate a plot twice that size, and 8 panels accommodate a 96 or 100 sq. ft. plot. Procedures for cutting panels from different types of welded wire are shown on the following page. Cages with an even number of panels will fold flat if the panels are of equal size. If an odd number of panels are used, one hinge wire must be removed to permit the cages to fold flat.

Below are diagrams of four cage structures produced by varying the number of panels. For these cages, the basic panel would be of welded 4 by 4-inch wire mesh cut to the following dimensions: base, 5 feet; height, 5 feet; top, 32 inches. Areas enclosed by circles within each diagram (left to right) correspond to plots of 4.8, 9.6, 19.2, and 96 square feet, respectively.

Slope of cage sides

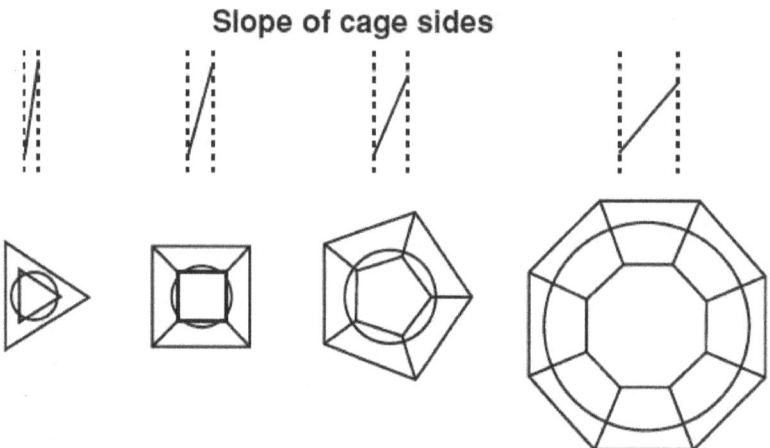

Cage Type 1 (continued)

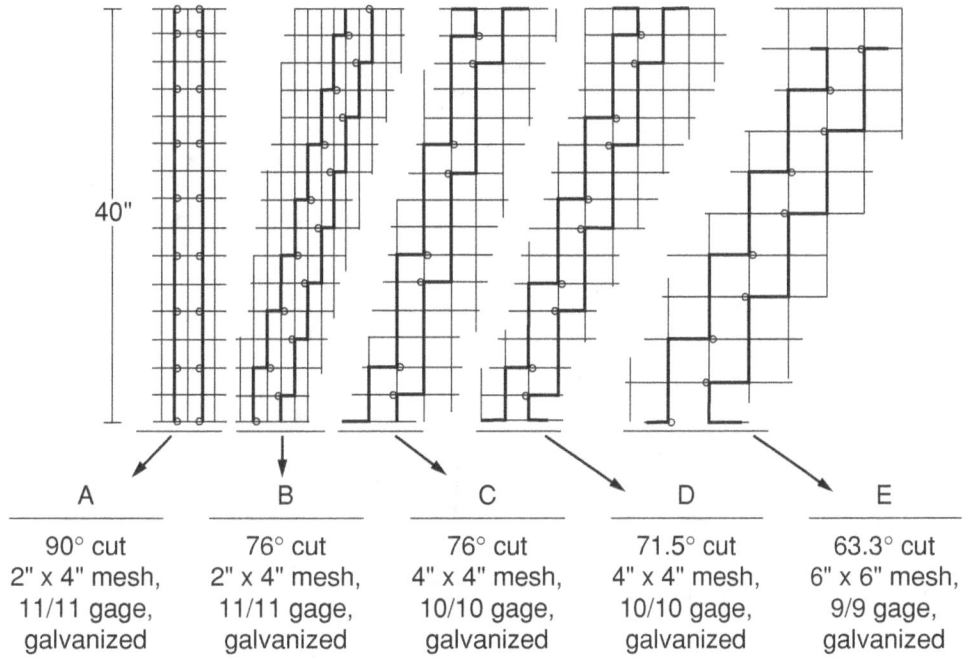

A	B	C	D	E
90° cut	76° cut	76° cut	71.5° cut	63.3° cut
2" x 4" mesh,	2" x 4" mesh,	4" x 4" mesh,	4" x 4" mesh,	6" x 6" mesh,
11/11 gage,	11/11 gage,	10/10 gage,	10/10 gage,	9/9 gage,
galvanized	galvanized	galvanized	galvanized	galvanized

The above are diagrams for cutting 5- by 5-foot panels from three types of welded wire. Loops are formed from horizontal wires as shown—other wires between panels are cut off.

Cage Type 2

A rigid steel post cage can be constructed by driving four steel posts in the ground to mark off the area to be protected. Make the posts sturdy by bracing from one post to another around the perimeter of the cage. Encircle this frame with either net or barbed wire. These cages are very stable, but they are difficult to move.

Cage Type 3

Igloo-shaped wire cages are light in weight, low in cost, portable, and easily placed. The cages are made in sets of four and can be nested. Use 6-inch mesh, 39 inches high. Wire lighter than 11-1/2 gage is unsuitable. To make four nesting cages: lengths of field fence are cut with 23, 24, 25, and 26 meshes intact. Each length is formed into a cylindrical shape and fastened by using the cut ends as ties, except those of the three upper meshes. The horizontal wires of the three upper meshes are cut at intervals of 90 degrees so that four nearly equal flaps are formed. These are bent inward and wired by their cut ends to make the top and complete the cage. A fencing tool and 8-inch lineman's pliers are suitable tools. In use, four 18-inch stakes of 1/2-inch reinforcing iron are driven diagonally inward over the bottom wire so that the cage is held taut and close to the ground. Small mesh wire 1 foot high around the bottom of the cage will exclude rabbits.

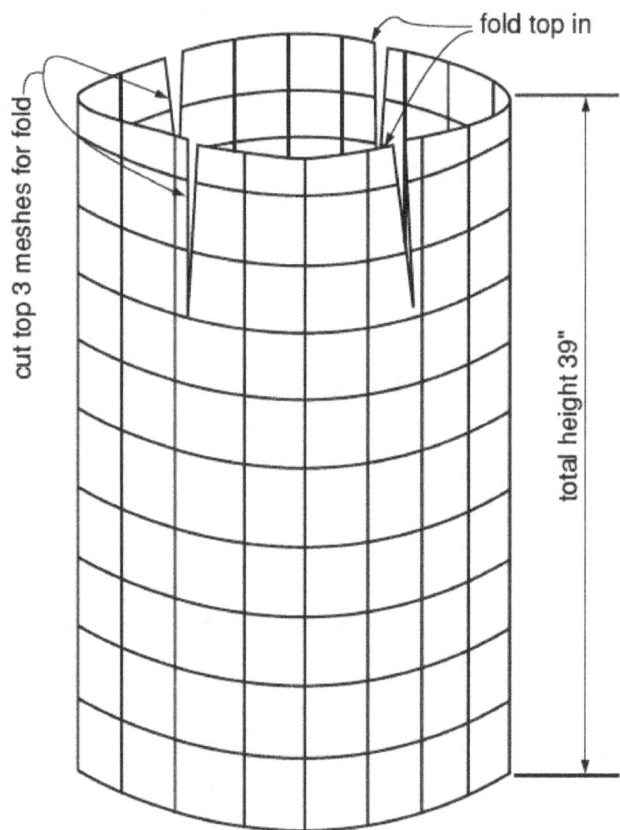

Cage Type 4

These cages are 4 feet square and are constructed of No. 9 galvanized wire. Every intersection is electronically welded. Cages are held in place with four pointed steel stakes, one on each side. These cages are easily transported from place to place and fold completely flat.

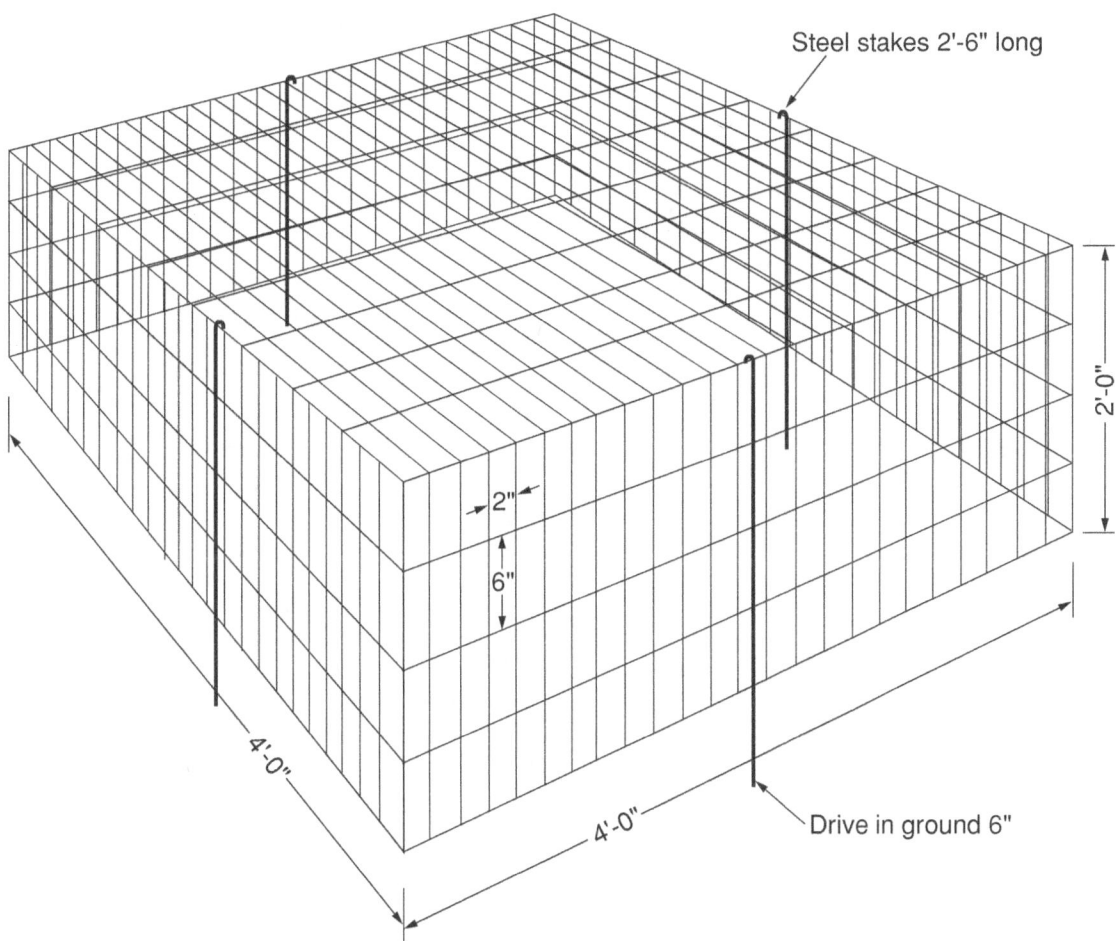

Steel stakes 2'-6" long

2"

6"

2'-0"

4'-0"

4'-0"

Drive in ground 6"

Cage Type 5

These cages are 4 feet by 5 feet at their base. They are constructed with 40 feet of 1/2-inch iron rod and 20 feet of 39-inch galvanized mesh wire. The size of the mesh is discretionary. The joints of the rod frame are welded and the wire is tied to the frame. The cages are held in place with four stakes that are at least 1 foot long, with hooks on the top. These cages are sturdy and are stackable for storage and transporting.

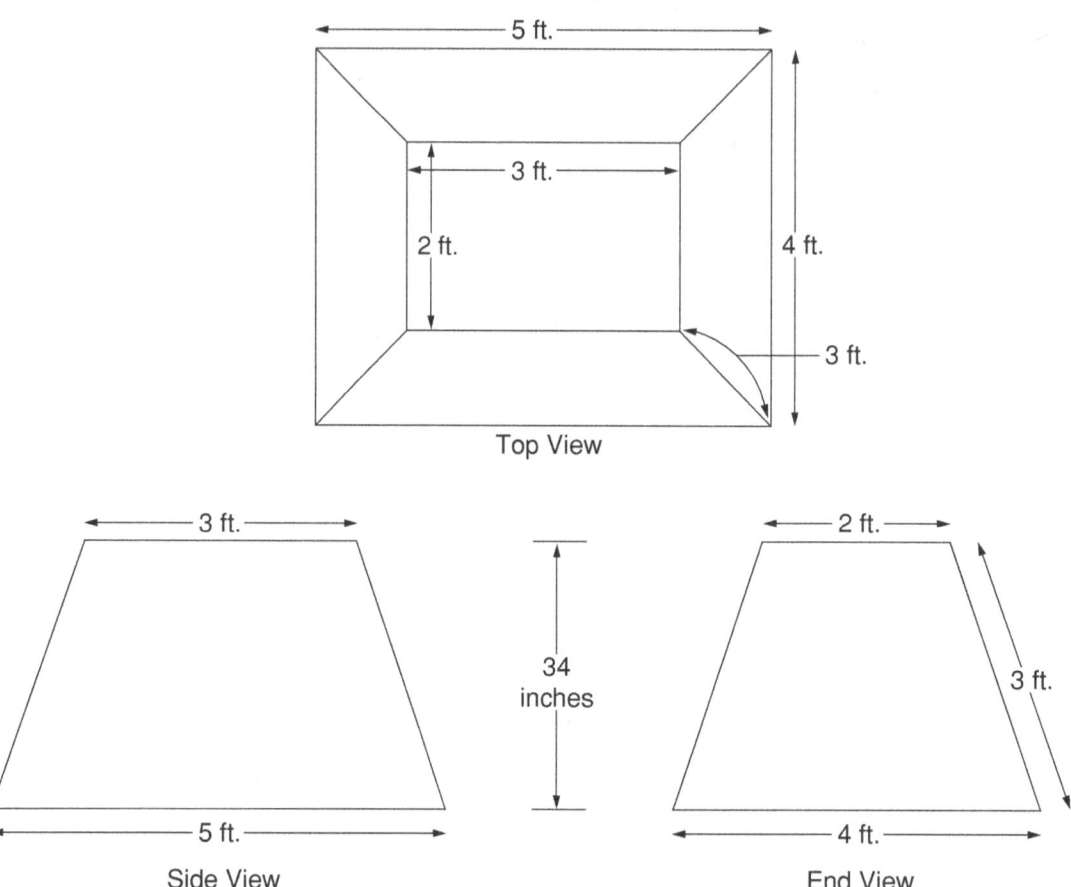

Top View

Side View

End View

Cage Type 6

These cages are about 4 feet square. They are constructed of prewelded mesh panels made with 1/4-inch rod. The sides of the cages are made by cutting a 32-inch x 16-foot mesh panel (hog panel) into four equal parts. The top is one-fourth of a 52-inch x 16-foot mesh panel. An acetylene torch can be used to cut the panels to the desired length. The cut ends are bent into different hooks that hold the cages together. Three types of panels are used for the sides of the cages and one for the top. This type of cage can be assembled in less than 5 minutes. The corners all lock together and do not have to be wired. Steel posts should be put on two sides of each cage to prevent livestock from pushing it around. Construction is strong enough to withstand cattle rubbing.

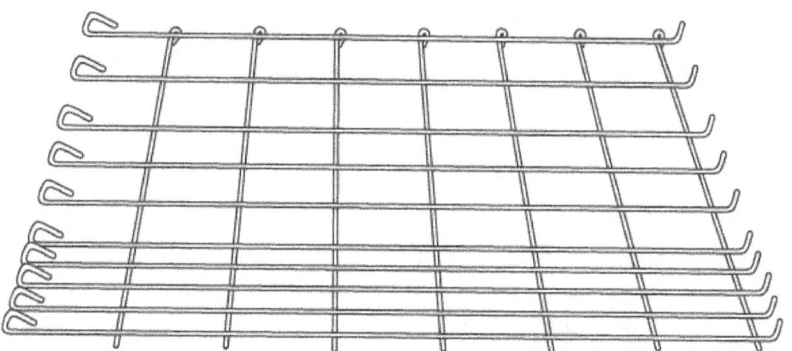

Figure 1

Panel type 1 (32 inches x about 4 feet).
One of these panels is needed for each cage. Note the hook design on both ends of this panel (corner hooks on the left and closing hooks on the right).

Figure 2

Panel type 2 (32 inches x about 4 feet).
Two of these panels are needed for each cage. Note the hook design (corner hooks) on the left end of the panel.

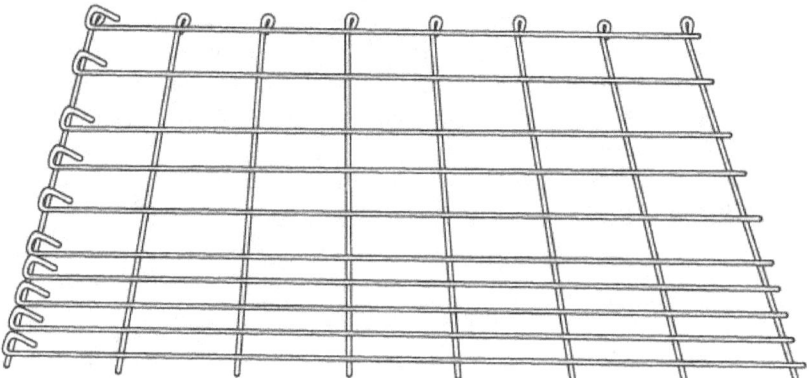

Figure 3

Panel type 3 (32 inches x about 4 feet).
This is the closing panel. One of these panels is needed for each cage. Note the hook design (closing hooks) on the left end of this panel. The right angle hooks on this panel and those shown on the panel in Picture 1 overlap to form a channel for a rebar rod to be thrust through to close the cage as shown in Picture 7.

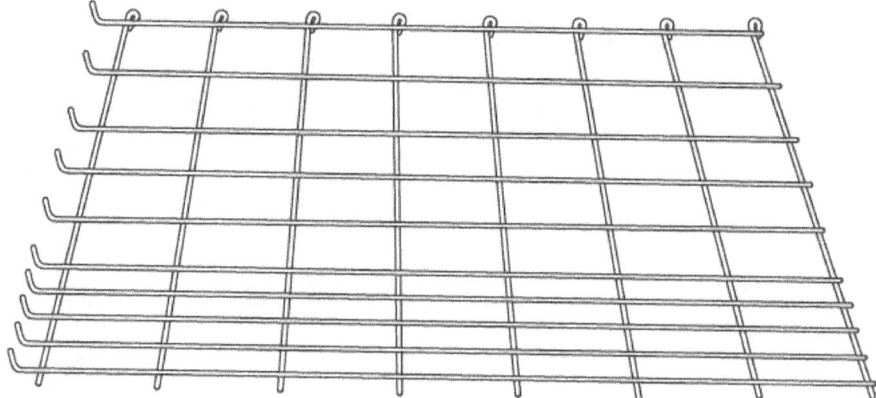

Figure 4

Top panel (about 4 feet square). One of these panels is needed for each cage. Note the hook design along two sides of this panel.

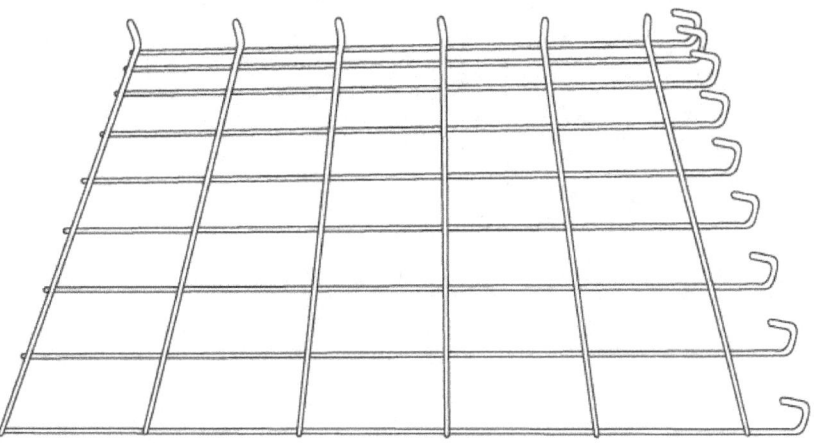

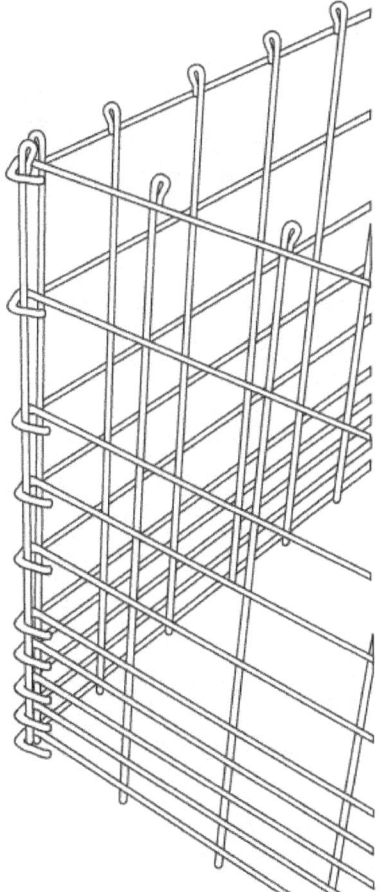

Figure 5

Shows how two panels are locked together using the corner hooks. Three corners of the cage will look like this. Note that the hooks are on the outside of the cage.

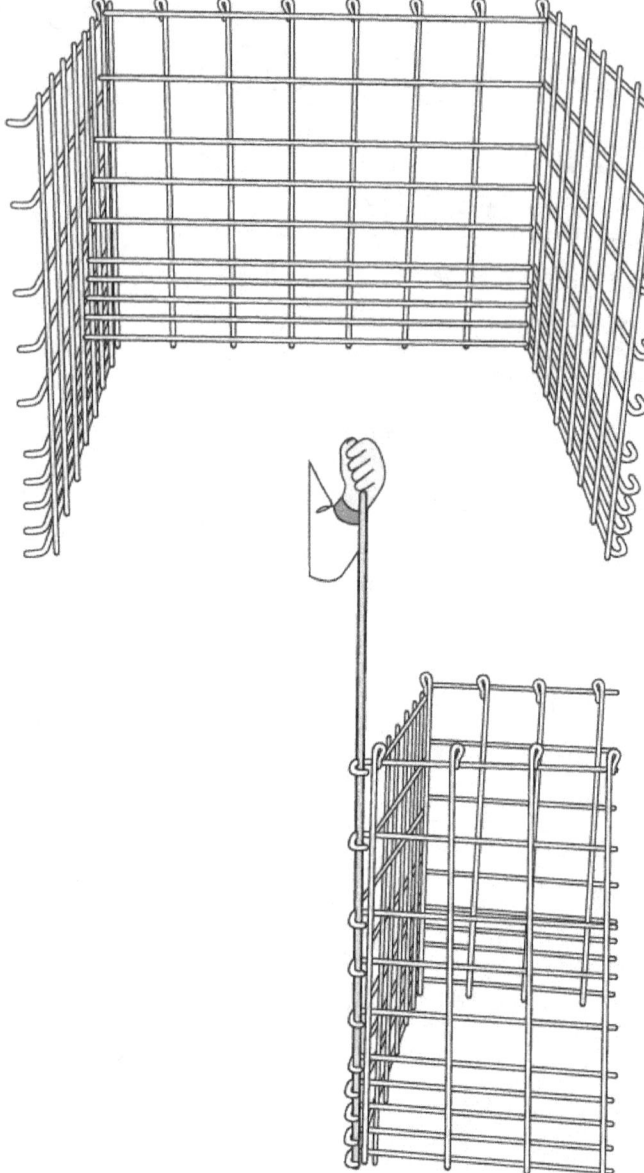

Figure 6

Shows three panels (panel type 1 on the left, panel type 2 in the center and on the right) locked together. The cage is ready to have the closing panel (panel type 3) put in place.

Figure 7

Shows how the closing panel (panel type 3) is locked to panel type 1 with a rebar rod being thrust through the closing hooks. The rod can be long enough to extend into the ground if desired.

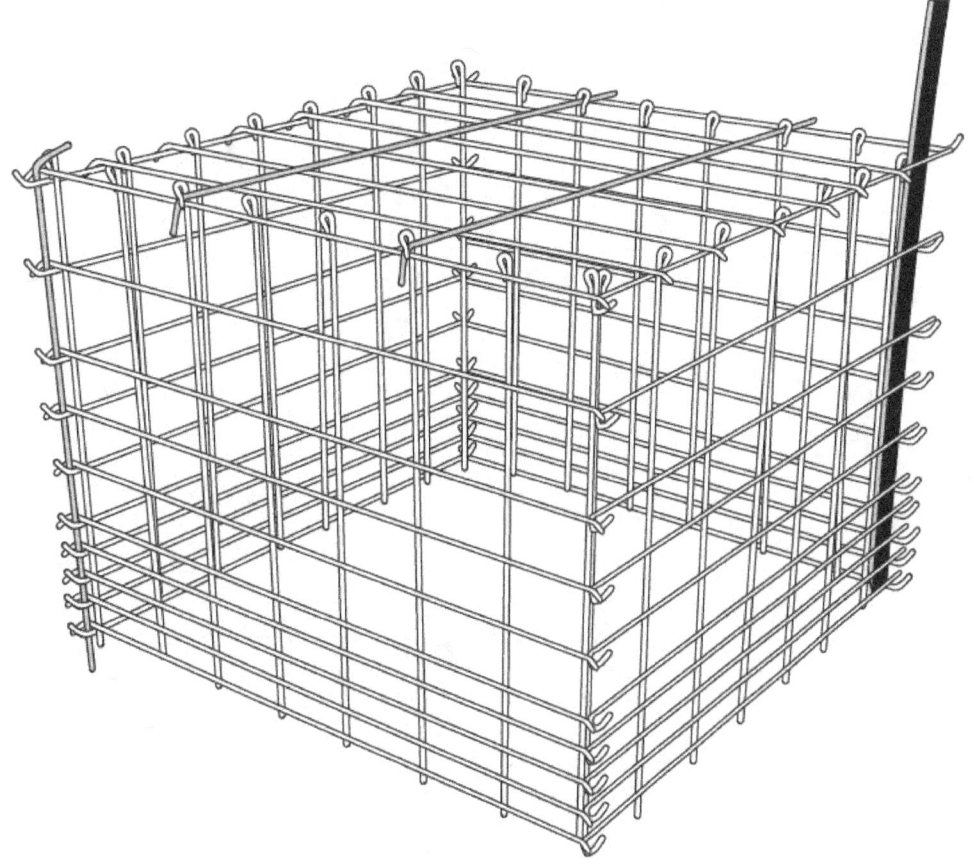

Figure 8

Completely assembled cage. The top panel is hooked on one side of the cage, laid across the cage, and held in place with two 1/4-inch locking rods pushed through loops along the top of the side panels of the cage.

APPENDIX F—
SELECTING RANDOM SAMPLES

Selecting random points along a baseline from which to run transects:

1. *Select Direction* If the baseline bisects the middle of the sample area, the first determination for selecting the location of a transect is to determine the direction each transect will be run perpendicular to the baseline. A simple flip of a coin could be used. Another way of selecting directions is to arbitrarily decide that odd numbers represent transects to the right of the baseline and even numbers represent transects to the left of the baseline. If five transects are required along a 100-meter baseline, start at some arbitrary point anywhere on the random digit table below and select the first five single digit numbers from left to right. As an example, the process could begin with the number sequence in row 15, column 4 (22695). Transects 1, 2, and 3 would be run to the left (numbers 2, 2, and 6), and transects 4 and 5 would be run to the right (9 and 5).

2. *Select Location* To select the location of each transect along the baseline, again start at some arbitrary point on the table of random numbers. In this case, use two-digit sequences. If row 19, column 3, is selected as the starting point, the five two-digit sequences would be 33, 52, 15, 56, and 37. Transects would be run at the 15-, 33-, 37-, 52-, and 56- meter marks along the baseline. Care should be taken to ensure that adjoining transect do not overlap. Depending on the ecological site and vegetation community, any interval can be selected as the minimum distance between transects. In this case, 10 meters has been established as the distance between transects. In the above example, the second and third transects (at the 33- and 37- meter marks) are within 10 meters of each other on the same side of the baseline. If they were to be run in opposite directions, there would be no problem. Since they are to be run in the same direction, discard the transect at the 37-meter mark and select the next two-digit sequence. A transect at the 39-meter mark (the next two digits in the table) is still within 10 meters of the previous transect. Continue the process until all transects are separated by 10 meters. With the next two-digit number sequence being 78, transect locations are now at the 15-, 33-, 52-, 56-, and 78-meter marks. Since the new third and fourth transects (52 and 56) are in opposite directions, the five transect locations have been determined.

   The table of random numbers could also be used for baselines over 100 meters. If the baseline is 200 meters, use a three-digit sequence to select the location of each transects. Only those three-digit numbers that fall between 1 and 200 would be used. This method requires the selection of many numbers because most will not fall between 1 and 200.

   There is a more efficient method of selecting random samples, particularly for two-, three-, and higher-digit numbers. To use this method, the random numbers must be treated as decimals. In our set of random digits, we would simply place a decimal point in front of every group of five digits and treat each group as one random number. Thus, if we entered the table at row 26, column 7, and read across, we would have the following six random numbers: 0.32978, 0.59902,

0.05463, 0.09245, 0.37631, and 0.74016. If we used a random number generator, it would be even easier since these provide random numbers as decimals falling between 0 and 1.

The formula for using these decimal random numbers for selecting a sampling unit or point is:

$$[u \times N] + 1$$

Where: u = Random number (expressed as decimal)
         N = Total population size
        [ ] = Used to indicate that only the integer part of the product is used in the calculation

To illustrate how this formula works, let's say that our baseline is 200 meters long. Here we need to select numbers between 0 and 200 as points along a baseline. Consider these points as a "population" of 200 possible points. Using the first of the six random numbers we came up with above, 0.32978, we calculate:

    [0.32978 x 200] + 1
= [65.956] + 1
= 65 + 1
= 66

Thus, 66 is the first point. Using the second random number we have:

    [0.59902 x 200] + 1
= [119.80400] + 1
= 119 + 1
= 120

Now we have the second point, 120. We continue in this manner until we have the five points we need. Although the formula may look difficult, a hand-held calculator or computer program with a random number generator makes it easy. The reason for adding the 1 to the integer of the product of the random number and N is that only whole numbers will be used. Without adding 1, it would be impossible to obtain the number 200. Consider the highest possible random number we could obtain, 0.99999. If we multiply this number by 200, we obtain 199.99800; taking the whole integer of this number yields the number 199. Adding 1 makes it 200.

As a rule of thumb, you should make sure the random numbers have more digits on the right side of the decimal point than the number of digits in N. In the example above, N is 200 and we are using random numbers with five digits to the right of the decimal point, so we are okay.

Note that this process is much more efficient than the first method because we do not need to reject any numbers. Given the fact that there is only a 1 in 5 chance of any three-digit number falling between 1 and 200, we would—on the average— have to examine 25 three-digit numbers to come up with five points under the first method. Using the second method, on the other hand, we can use the first five random numbers from the table to select the same five points.

Table of Random Digits (Zar 1984)

	00-04	05-09	10-14	15-19	20-24	25-29	30-34	35-39	40-44	45-49
00	22808	04391	45529	53968	57136	98228	85485	13801	68194	56382
01	49305	36965	44849	64987	59501	35141	50159	57369	76913	75739
02	81934	19920	73316	69243	69605	17022	53264	83417	55193	92929
03	10840	13508	48120	22467	54505	70536	91206	81038	22418	34800
04	99555	73289	59605	37105	24621	44100	72832	12268	97089	68112
05	32677	45709	62337	35132	45128	96761	08745	53388	98353	46724
06	09401	75407	27704	11569	52842	83543	44750	03177	50511	15301
07	73424	31711	65519	74069	56744	40864	75315	89066	96563	75142
08	37075	81378	59472	71858	86903	66860	03757	32723	54273	45477
09	02060	37158	55244	44812	45369	78939	08048	28036	40946	03898
10	94719	43565	40028	79866	43137	28063	52513	66405	71511	66135
11	70234	48272	59621	88778	16536	36505	41724	24776	63971	01685
12	07972	71752	92745	86465	01845	27416	50519	48458	68460	63113
13	58521	64882	26993	48104	61307	73933	17214	44827	88306	78177
14	32580	45202	21148	09684	39411	04892	02055	75276	51831	85686
15	88796	30829	35009	22695	23694	11220	71006	26720	39476	60538
16	31525	82746	78935	82980	61236	28940	96341	13790	66247	33839
17	02747	35989	70387	89571	34570	17002	79223	96817	31681	15207
18	46651	28987	20525	61347	63981	41085	67412	29053	00724	14841
19	43598	14436	33521	55637	39789	26560	66404	71802	18763	80560
20	30596	92319	11474	64546	60030	73795	60809	24016	29166	36059
21	56198	64370	85771	62633	78240	05766	32419	35769	14057	80674
22	68266	67544	06464	84956	18431	04015	89049	15098	12018	89338
23	31107	28597	65102	75599	17496	87590	68848	33021	69855	54015
24	37555	05069	38680	87274	55152	21792	77219	48732	03377	01160
25	90463	27249	43845	94391	12145	36882	48906	52336	00780	74407
26	99189	88731	93531	52638	54989	04237	32978	59902	05463	09245
27	37631	74016	89072	59598	55356	27346	80856	80875	52850	36548
28	73829	21651	50141	76142	72303	06694	61697	76662	23745	96282
29	15634	89428	47090	12094	42134	62301	87236	90110	53463	46969
30	00571	45172	78532	63863	98597	15742	41967	11821	91389	07476
31	83374	10184	56384	27050	77700	13875	96607	76479	80535	17454
32	78666	85645	13181	08700	08289	62956	54439	39150	95690	18555
33	47890	88197	21358	65254	35917	54035	83028	84636	38186	50581
34	56238	13559	79344	83198	94542	35165	40188	21456	67024	62771
35	35369	32234	38129	59963	99237	72648	66504	99065	61161	16186
36	42934	34578	28968	74028	42164	55647	76805	61023	33099	48293
37	09010	15226	43474	30174	26727	39317	48508	55438	85336	40762
38	83897	90073	72941	85613	85569	24183	08247	15946	02957	68504
39	82206	01230	93252	89045	25141	91943	75531	87420	99012	80751
40	14175	32992	49046	41272	94040	44929	98531	27712	05106	35242
41	58968	88367	70927	74765	18635	85122	27722	95388	61523	91745
42	62601	04595	76926	11007	67631	64641	07994	04639	39314	83126
43	97030	71165	47032	85021	65554	66774	21560	04121	57297	85415
44	89074	31587	21360	41673	71192	85795	82157	52928	62586	02179
45	07806	81312	81215	99858	26762	28993	74951	64680	50934	32011
46	91540	86466	13229	76624	44092	96604	08590	89705	03424	48033
47	99279	27334	33804	77988	93592	90708	56780	70097	39907	51006
48	63224	05074	83941	25034	43516	22840	35230	66048	80754	46302
49	98351	97513	27529	65419	35328	19738	82366	38573	50967	72754

REPORT DOCUMENTATION PAGE

Form Approved
OMB No. 0704-0188

1. AGENCY USE ONLY *(Leave blank)*	2. REPORT DATE August 1996	3. REPORT TYPE AND DATES COVERED Final

4. TITLE AND SUBTITLE

Utilization Studies and Residual Measurements

5. FUNDING NUMBERS

6. AUTHOR(S)

Interagency Technical Team

7. PERFORMING ORGANIZATION NAME(S) AND ADDRESS(ES)

U.S. Department of the Interior
Bureau of Land Management - National Applied Resource Sciences Center
P.O. Box 25047
Denver, CO 80225-0047

8. PERFORMING ORGANIZATION REPORT NUMBER

BLM/RS/ST-96/004+1730

9. SPONSORING/MONITORING AGENCY NAME(S) AND ADDRESS(ES)

10. SPONSORING/MONITORING AGENCY REPORT NUMBER

11. SUPPLEMENTARY NOTES

12a. DISTRIBUTION/AVAILABILITY STATEMENT

12b. DISTRIBUTION CODE

13. ABSTRACT *(Maximum 200 words)*

This interagency technical reference provides the basis for consistent, uniform, and standard utilization studies and residual measurements that are economical, repeatable, statistically reliable, and technically adequate. While not all inclusive, this reference does include the primary study methods used across the West (twig length measurement, stubble height, comparative yield, paired plot, ocular estimate, key species, height-weight, etc.).

14. SUBJECT TERMS

- Rangeland inventory
- Rangeland monitoring
- Rangeland evaluation
- Utilization studies
- Residual measurements

15. NUMBER OF PAGES

176, including covers

16. PRICE CODE

17. SECURITY CLASSIFICATION OF REPORT Unclassified	18. SECURITY CLASSIFICATION OF THIS PAGE Unclassified	19. SECURITY CLASSIFICATION OF ABSTRACT Unclassified	20. LIMITATION OF ABSTRACT UL

NSN 7540-01-280-5500

Standard Form 298 (Rev. 2-89)
Prescribed by ANSI Std. Z39-18
298-102